BREAKING CARDINAL RULES
Basketball and the Escort Queen

Katina Powell
with
Dick Cady

Published & distributed by:

IBJ Book Publishing, LLC
41 E. Washington St., Suite 200
Indianapolis, IN 46204
www.ibjbp.com

Certified Fraud & Forensic Investigation (CFFI), Indianapolis, Indiana,
provided mobile forensic services.
wecatchfraud.com

ISBN 978-1-939550-28-6
Library of Congress Control Number: 2015948793
First Edition
Printed in the United States of America

Much of this story is extracted from Katina Powell's diary/journal entries. Whenever possible, the language has been preserved, with minor changes for clarity or grammar. Readers should be aware that some material is raw, graphic, and shocking. We have also used, as much as possible, direct quotes from interviews conducted for the purpose of explanation or amplification. Two dancers, TooTall and Coco, asked that their names be changed. In her journals Katina refers to the other dancers by their stage names.

In every sense, then, this is Katina Powell's story. Or maybe "Bam's" story. Many people know her by that nickname. But it isn't the only name she has used.

~ Editors

KATINA'S ESCORT RULES

1. NO hot hotels. Quality (Inn), Best Westerns, Hurstbourne, Ramada, Super 8
   YES hotels. Red Roof, Extended Stay
2. Circle the parking lot
3. Never Say Price, Rate or Money. I take donations for my time and companionship. For the half hour $150 donations, $200 to the house
4. Don't answer door for strange people
5. Meet them in Exit ALWAYS!!
6. Never meet in the lobby!!!! EVER!!
   If it don't seem right then it's NOT right. Go with gut feeling
8. Never take a check!! EVER!!

I FELT LIKE I WAS PART OF THE RECRUITMENT TEAM.
A LOT OF THEM PLAYERS WENT TO LOUISVILLE
BECAUSE OF ME.

-Katina Powell

Sometimes a perfectly ordinary day will unexpectedly open the door to perfectly extraordinary things.

On a perfectly ordinary day in 2010, Katina Powell went to visit her friend Tink, who, like her, lived and worked in what some would call the mean streets in the west end of Louisville, Kentucky.

In her late thirties and not happy about it, Katina was a single mother of three daughters struggling to find ways to make more money. Just recently, she thought she might have turned the corner. She'd always known men wanted her body, and she liked plenty of sex herself. Now, like waking up to the snap of a hypnotist's fingers, she'd had a revelation. Men not only would pay for sex, some men were eager to pay, no questions asked.

Easy money? A guy who owned a store in her neighborhood, a man she called The Arab, handed over one hundred dollars for three minutes of her time. Wham, bam, thank you, ma'am, indeed. No overhead, no taxes, no complaints, no regrets. Sugar for sugar.

Always ready to run with, if not exploit, an idea, Katina started working for Cheetah's Escort Service. Good money could be had, but not necessarily steady money. Of everything she took in, she had to give sixty percent to Cheetah's owner, and she was trying to figure out a way to get around that. She also started something she was proud of, a dance troupe that put on sexy shows in clubs and at occasional bachelor parties. The women were mostly unmarried friends of hers, good-looking party girls who didn't mind strip-teasing.

1

Naturally, a girl could pick up extra cash by giving customers the satisfaction they sought after becoming thoroughly inflamed watching a half-dozen chocolate-skinned babes flaunting their goodies.

Tink was an intimate friend. He had a barber shop where the smell of marijuana wasn't unknown. At the time the shop was called Cardinal Kuts. Tink was an avid University of Louisville fan, and his customers included some players from the school.

He was the kind of man Katina could talk to about anything. Usually, when Katina came by to see what was happening, one or two of the guys who hung around the shop made a play for her, always without success. "No thanks, nigga," Katina snapped. She had a boyfriend she loved dearly. The sex business was just that—business.

On this day, Tink had a proposal of his own. An unusual proposal.

A very unusual proposal.

How would you like to have your girls dance for some of the players at the U of L?

Are you kidding? When?

Tink knew Andre McGee, a graduate assistant working for Coach Rick Pitino in the University of Louisville's storied basketball program. McGee wanted the girls to entertain some of the players and potential recruits.

How many girls you need?

Many as you can get. It's worth $300, plus tips.

Understand, like many Louisville residents and other Kentucky residents, Katina loved Cardinal basketball, worshipped the young black superstars who made up most of the team—they were celebrities, really—and thought Coach Pitino should have the Basketball Hall of Fame named after him.

It didn't matter that the coach recently had been caught up in a nasty scandal where a woman, now the divorced wife of Pitino's equipment manager, had been found guilty of trying to extort

$10 million from him based on a 2003 sexual encounter and abortion. The school had stood by its prized coach.

To an inner-city girl who had dropped out of Catholic high school and was struggling to earn her GED, the 21,000-student University of Louisville was a kind of monolithic centerpiece in a separate world all its own, a world of brains, money, academic achievement, and national sports glory, especially on the basketball court.

She also knew something about McGee. Out of California, only twenty-three now, he had been starting point guard for the Cardinals for four seasons. He was 5 foot 10, a muscular 180 pounds, and a slick scorer. Twice his Cards had made it to the Elite Eight in the NCAA tournament. He had played one year of pro ball in Germany before Pitino took him on to help handle and guide the players.

The responsibilities of his job included assisting in "on-campus recruiting efforts."

Among major universities, recruiting competition is fierce. The revenues are enormous—Louisville's basketball income is one of the highest in the country, and Pitino is one of the highest-paid coaches. In basketball programs, highly touted potential recruits are wooed like young princes and treated like celebrities. Victories, national glory and millions of dollars sometimes will hinge on the decisions, or perhaps whims, of adolescents still in high school.

In 2010, for example, Pitino put a priority on signing McDonald's All-American guard Rodney Purvis from North Carolina. Sought by half a dozen other large universities, Purvis visited Louisville and verbally committed to play there, partly because a man he knew had joined Pitino's staff. Not six months later, Purvis de-committed and chose North Carolina State because his friend had taken another job. Purvis did not participate in Katina's activities.

With her visit set up for an approaching evening, Katina had no problem rounding up dancers—girls with stage names like Meka,

Skyy, Honey and Amber, while Katina danced using the name Platinum. They were eager, even thrilled. They gathered up their skimpy costumes—spangled bras, thongs, sequined bikini panties and the like—and piled into the car.

The University of Louisville! Basketball stars! It would be a night to remember.

Or maybe the first of many nights to remember.

The event was to be held at the dormitory where many of the players lived under McGee's putative supervision. The Billy Minardi Hall, near the Greek houses on South Fourth Street, is a two-story brick building named in honor of Pitino's brother-in-law, one of the World Trade Center victims on 9/11. The facility has one-and two-bedroom suites, a learning center, lounge and recreation room. For the students who pay to stay there, a double-room starts at around $3,000 a semester. McGee had his own rooms.

It was part of the main campus, though not in the noisy, nosy heart of everything. It had a parking lot and a drive behind the building. The front and back had double doors, opened with key cards, which were monitored sometimes by a single security guard. The building also had a convenient, let us say discreet, single door

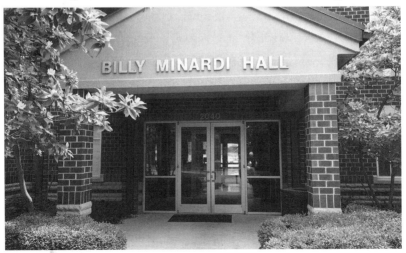

Dorm where the men's basketball team resided

4

around the side, through which special night-time visitors could be escorted, say five or six attractive and obviously excited women.

The first of many nights to remember began with excitement, all right. That evening, leaving from the parking lot was star Cardinal point guard Preston Knowles, who had finished the 2009-2010 season as the Big East leader in three-point shooting percentage. It was like seeing a movie star in the flesh.

McGee met the women at the side door.

He was flamboyant:

"I'm McGee, how you doing?
The girls look good."

They went into an empty dorm room.

Katina related in her journal:

> *I'd never been there before. The rooms were like a living*
> *room with two bedrooms with bathrooms, like a barracks.*
> *The players were in another room.*

Katina's girls thought the night couldn't have gone better. Katina didn't think it would be repeated.

Dancers' side door entrance of Billy Minardi Hall

But this would be the first of nearly two dozen outings, all following a similar routine.

> *McGee was in control of a lot when it came to the dorm. Andre told me how he wanted it done, but usually it was for me to send the girls out one at a time. There were seven or eight players and music from an iPod with speakers. Andre played this one song 'Racks on racks' (money on money) by rapper YC that drove the girls nuts - they were so sick of it. The girls stripped down to nothing. They were my friends, so they were willing to do it. While they were dancing, Andre would find out which dancer each recruit and player wanted to have sex with. Then he would work a side-deal with me to negotiate the price. Usually $100-$120 each. Pay was always upfront. Andre paid me and I paid the girls on the spot. After the dancing, some of them went into other rooms with players.*

It wasn't just players and recruits who enjoyed this kind of entertainment. So did some of their fathers. Of one, Katina recalled:

> *The Dad said he more than likely will send his son to Louisville due to the "more than extra" activities. He said he will call in the morning for two dancers if he has time before he leaves.*

At the peak of the dormitory and off-campus entertainment more than $10,000 cash changed hands to Katina for supplying the women. This does not include the hundreds of one dollar bills thrown at the dancers at each party by McGee, the recruits and players. Nor does it include the money paid to the women who had sex with the recruits afterward.

So frequent were the escapades that Katina would later say, especially after the Cardinals won the 2012-2013 NCAA championship:

> *I felt like I was part of the recruitment team. A lot of them players went to Louisville because of me.*

If Katina deserved some sort of whispered, back-handed credit for her illicit and decidedly erotic services, so did her three daughters. All of them worked for or with her in the sex trade.

PEOPLE MAY THINK THAT I EXPOSE MY KIDS.
BUT, SHIT, THEY ENJOY THEMSELVES;
THEY MEET NEW PEOPLE... FOR THOSE WHO HAVE
A PROBLEM WIT' THIS, KISS MY ASS.

-Katina Powell

Across America it is likely more than one mother has nudged or pushed a daughter into renting out her body.

The Four Horsemen of Our Apocalypse—greed, poverty, drugs and alcohol—have a way of shoving morality into the nearest dark closet with the hope that it won't come out while the money's still coming in.

Certainly it's at least possible some misguided or sociopathic mother has sent a second daughter along the proverbial primrose path of prostitution.

But three daughters, working with Mom at times without recrimination, and certainly without apology?

> *People may think that I expose my kids. But, shit, they enjoy themselves, they meet new people. Believe me, they have their own lives, but they enjoy the perks of shows. For those who have a problem wit' this, kiss my ass.*

To understand how this could happen—to the extent it can be understood—you must try to understand Katina Powell.

Knowing about her helps explain how she became a kind of clandestine, off-the-books, recruiting assistant for the University of Louisville as she arranged 22 night-time parties at the men's basketball dormitory or other places over nearly four years.

The answers, in part, can be found in journals or diaries Katina kept to record her life in the sex trade, her thoughts, her fears, and her dreams. These outpourings fill most of five books with a

9

Shows in 2010 (2011) (2012) (2013)
End OF

Didn't really caculate or recorded or
(documented shows this early on
Most of my 2010 shows were for U of L
Basketball team.
(2013)

2011 – Terrance Williams –	$ 500.00	BBT U of L – $350.00
Fire fighter –	$ 200.00	BBT U of L – $600.00
Magic –	$ 140.00	Vision 1 – $300.00
U of L – Basketball	$ 300.00	Pewee – $240.00
U of L – Basketball	$ 300.00	Coles – $250.00
Cops –	$ 500.00	Coles – $250.00
U of L – Basketball	$ 300.00	U of L – $250.00
Cops –	$ 200.00	Fella – $300.00
U of L – Basketball	$ 300.00	
U of L – Basketball	$ 200.00	
U of L – Basketball	$ 200.00	
U of L Basketball	$ 250.00	
U of L Basketball	$ 300.00	
Crazy Joe Business	$ 300.00 + $200	
U of L Basketball	$ 300.00	
U of L Basketball	$ 300.00	
Arab –	$ 100.00	
Terrance Williams	$ 1000.00	
U of L – McGee	$ 120.00	
McGee's people.	$ 300.00	
Bachelor Party	$ 300.00	
Tink's Bachelor Party	$ 300.00	
U of L Basketball	$ 400.00	
U of L Basketball	$ 400.00	
Crazy Joe Business	$ 500.00	
U of L Basketball	$ 300.00	
U of L Basketball	$ 300.00	
U of L Basketball	$ 350.00	

Page in one of Katina's journals showing 19 of 22 U of L shows

story that is alternately fascinating and repelling, brutally candid, narcissistic, sometimes poignant, sometimes pitiable.

Besides details of outings at the University of Louisville, they provide an unvarnished, and perhaps unprecedented, look inside part of what authorities call America's $1 billion-a-year escort business.

Nowhere in them will you find an act of redemption or a bracing moral lesson. Sex is a natural currency. Marijuana is almost always near at hand.

This is a woman full of contradictions. Katina could be hot or cold with customers as the need dictated, but she was always romantically passionate, and ferociously jealous, with her long-time boyfriend.

She might at one point work with her daughters peddling sex— and take them to church the next day. At times she prayed to God, occasionally with the hope that God would drum up more business. Sometimes an entry in one of her journals will be a poem or song— followed soon enough by a spite-filled, obscenity-laced diatribe against some girlfriend or rival.

In a sense, the strangest contradiction is this: Although Katina is from certain drug-ridden streets of Louisville, her life could have been—perhaps should have been—much different.

Hers undoubtedly was a happy childhood. She wasn't a ghetto kid from a broken home. She wasn't molested or otherwise abused. No one pushed or forced her in the direction she went. She more or less made her own way. For part of her adult life, she had worked a variety of indifferent or menial jobs, including cleaning houses and apartments. Selling sex offered the possibility of an income of which she had only dreamed.

Odd as it sounds, she approached various aspects of the sex business with a calculating, entrepreneurial spirit. Today, a 43-year-old grandmother, she's smart, literate, a quick thinker, able to play roles as circumstances dictate, and often bubbling over with ideas. Certainly she isn't lazy; far from it.

Born in 1972, the third youngest of eight children, she doted on her father, a hard-working foreman for the city parks department.

Her mother, a loving woman who tried to provide a normal upbringing for her family, died of breast cancer when Katina was in her early teens. Growing up, the children played with friends, had dogs, rabbits and hamsters, and always had plenty to eat.

"I was young. I didn't understand it," Katina said of her mother's death. Any pain was eased by her father's love. *"I was really close to my father."*

Her father did a good job playing the role of a single parent, Katina recalled. He also kept her busy after her mother's death, by making her step up "really quick" in helping manage the household and her siblings.

Although Katina's father didn't go to church, the family prayed at meals and on other occasions. She went to St. Columba Catholic School. As part of the First Communion ceremony she swore to renounce Satan. In the eighth grade she played basketball. She graduated to Holy Cross High School. Briefly, she took journalism classes.

That was the child who dreamed of becoming a superstar, perhaps a dancer, maybe a millionaire.

She would end up fulfilling one of those dreams, though not quite in the way she would have imagined back then.

The adult she grew into has used many names—Bam, Platinum, Ashley, Crystal,

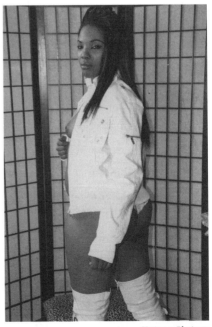

Katina as Platinum

12

Kream, Jazzmine, to name a few. Over recent years, some two dozen women have worked with her or for her. They danced in clubs and private parties, and some worked as escorts. Men on the prowl could find them through different kinds of sexy or alluring advertising, including the Internet service Backpage.com.

The mindset that brought this about had formed by high school, where Katina wasn't a very good student. She resisted authority and stubbornly had to have the last word. She got pregnant in her junior year and dropped out. She was married, divorced with three children, each daughter by a different man. For years she's smoked marijuana regularly, often several "blunts" (thick cigarettes) a day.

Although the Powell family enjoyed considerable stability, their lives didn't entirely reflect the artificial comfort and familial connections they could see in TV shows like "Full House." Their home, thanks to their parents, was a kind of safe zone—she calls it a protective "shell"—in the urban jungle.

Around where they lived were various forms of temptation, drug-dealing chief among them. With drug-dealers comes violence. In time, guns were like magnets to the Powell boys.

Her older brother, known as Pete, has been jailed numerous times, including for accidentally shooting a woman during a fight. When Pete's son was murdered in 2011—he was shot multiple times and killed—it devastated the whole family.

Things got worse for Pete in August 2015, when police alleged he and another man used a lead pipe to beat a woman they'd been offered $1,500 to attack.

Katina's brother Deshawn, nicknamed Rock, also has a long police record and was shot and wounded eight times during an incident that occurred in the summer of 2015. One sister shunned the family to the point where she told others her father was dead. A cousin has been locked up for shootings and theft.

Another cousin received an eighteen-year sentence for murder. Katina has no criminal record.

Estrangements in the family meant the end of traditional Thanksgiving dinners.

Family was an important element in her life, but the daughters she had were sired by three different men. None of these men was a factor in the child's life, early or later on. And so, Katina, a strong-willed woman, was their principal guide as they grew up.

Of the oldest, Lindsay, who was age 19 in 2010 when the shows at the University of Louisville started, Katina once wrote,

> *Ms. Lindsay, my first born, hard as a rock but has a heart of peanut butter. It took me a long time to break through to her. She was so rebellious that it was crazy.*

Her father was the nephew of one of Katina's brothers-in-law.

By age 16 Lindsay began to perform with her mother and other women in strip acts, and, eventually, at the college dormitory and as an escort. Katina once described Lindsay as "my crybaby bully child" who needed her love daily.

> *Lindsay is my daughter and also a team player. She does most of the shows. She started off picking up money* (thrown at the dancers by men, but not performing or having sex). *Now she does good. I think she likes it. It puts money in her pocket, plus it is fun.*

The second daughter, Rod-Ni, who was age 17 in 2010, soon followed. Her father only came around when Rod-Ni was 13 and when she was 16, he died in a hail of thirteen bullets when someone attempted to rob him. Katina would write:

> *Now Rod-Ni, whoa! That's my chick. She sees everything that I miss or don't see. She picks up money now that Lindsay has upgraded to a dancer. Niggas really like Rod-Ni.*

Of all the women who worked with or for Katina, Rod-Ni was one of the most attractive. She describes Rod-Ni as "my white child" for her mannerisms and tendency to hang with people who act white.

She's down to get money but not quite yet; she's still new to the game.

Perhaps it was inevitable that the third girl, Shay, who was age 15 in 2010, would follow her sisters as they had followed their mother into the trade that year.

Shay, my prize possession, my beautiful creation doesn't need much attention but a lot of watching.

Shay also proved to be the most rebellious. She did have an intermittent relationship with her father, but at 15, as Katina tried to get the man to pay some attention, Shay told her, "Mama, let it go."

Concern for her youngest child—that "one last hope" to apply one's parenting skills honed by mistakes made while rearing older children—weighed on Katina.

She once again demonstrates that she's a woman of contradictions. On one hand, here's a mother who allowed her three daughters to follow her down a dark career path just as a parent in the suburbs might suggest her young scion take a key role in the family's business.

Katina agonized as deeply as any other mother about wanting to see the best for her youngest daughter. A 2011 journal entry set forth in a heartfelt plea:

Lord, please give me the strength to not kill my child. I don't understand what I have done wrong. U know I try my best to back this child in everything she does. I can't blame her actions and disrespect on her bum-ass father. She knows right from wrong. I mean I was 16 before, so some things I understand, but I'm tired of it.

How dare she bring two niggas in my house and have sex with them, her and her friend. If it wasn't for the other

*parent I wouldn't allow that child back in my house. Now
their friendship is destroyed because of some dirty broke-ass
nigga. She's providing pussy and can't provide money to
pay her phone bill. These kids are asshole backwards. This
generation is sooo stupid, and the more you try to teach them
the dumber they get. Lord help them.*

A little later Katina lamented:

*I'm somewhat depressed. My youngest daughter feels as though
I have never done anything for her. I have only been doing for this
child since Day 1. Nobody else has sheltered and spoiled a child
as much as I have done with her. The other kids don't understand
why I don't give up on her while I have the chance. I know she has
the potential to be a good girl, but something is really blocking
her. I believe she is angry with me because of the lack of love
received from her father. I do my best to love her for the both of
us, but she feels like it ain't enough....*

Shay continued to disappoint Katina.

*I had a major slap in the face, I have never believed in a man
making money off of me or the giving forcefully of my money to a
pimp. My youngest daughter decided to go to New York with Lexi,
the same chick that got us started using Backpage.com to meet
men. She goes to New York and came back with a pimp.
I was disgusted with her and myself. They took her to
Lexington to escort, then made her give the money to them.
So basically her ass was doing it for free.*

And when Shay's pimp took her daughter to Miami...

*I felt helpless, embarrassed, and mad. Was this my fault?
It turned out Lexi had seven felonies and the mysterious pimp
was wanted in New York.*

My daughter was gone for a total of six long months.

I talked to her almost every other day, but that didn't really help. I needed to see her. Since doing this she has been robbed twice, once at gunpoint in New York and then again in Indianapolis. She took it as though it was nothing, I really think that she's locked in (to this lifestyle).

Shay participated in the shows at clubs and at the University of Louisville, but would continue to wind her way down a dangerous path.

THE LOOKS ON THESE KIDS' FACES WAS
SOMETIMES HEART-BREAKING, BECAUSE IT WAS ALL
TOO MUCH FOR THEM. THINK ABOUT IT.
YOU ARE A SENIOR IN HIGH SCHOOL AND YOU
GET THE OPPORTUNITY TO HAVE SEX WITH THESE
HIGHLY EXPERIENCED FEMALES.

-Katina Powell

About seven players attended the second outing at the University of Louisville basketball dorm. It also doubled as a kind of birthday party for Tink's cousin. Tink paid Katina. After that, she dealt exclusively with McGee.

Some of the women arrived wearing their skimpy costumes. McGee told them they had to be covered up when they entered the dorm. Yet within a short time, they were using the main entrance. The security guard never said a word. But he and some of the other students living in the dorm were aware of their presence.

By July of 2011 Katina would write in her diary:

> So here is how life is going. It's time for me to put on my third club show, the biggest ever!
>
> I've been putting on lil' private shows enough to get paid and eat pretty good. Since I have been doing shows I have come across some very interesting people. I've heard and also seen a lot of very strange things. I have dealt with U of L—Andre McGee, 'payee' is what I like to call him. That's my nigga holding it down.

Katina continued:

> I have dealt with more than a handful of new recruits. So I can say that I am partially responsible for them coming to U of L.
>
> Oh, and let's not leave out Mr. T-Will, yes, Mr. Terrence Williams, people. Believe me, as cocky and arrogant as he

was, he paid swell!! $500 for two girls. But my most popular one that I love to (have the) *shows for is my buddy 'Chane,'* (Behanan). *That boy has potential in every way.*

I have done shows for half of Louisville and plan to take over the other half. I'm already blessed with Beauty but it is so much more when you also have the 'Booty.'

Katina and Chane Behanan

Even as they looked forward to more work at U of L, Katina and her ladies kept busy. Of a day in August 2011 she wrote:

Bachelor party for Kentae, Tink's partner in the barber shop. I took Lindsay, TooTall, Keena and Dolly. I made money but it was a straight disaster. Keena's a bum bitch, stopped dancing because she wasn't making a lot of money. Dolly's nigga was trying to pay her and she just blew him off. Broke ass people. The bachelor got sick and threw up. You win some, you lose some.

The next day – I was asked to do a bachelor party by

20

Stephanie for her fiancé Jerry. I took Lindsay, TooTall, Cameo (friend of TooTall), Honey and Boobie. Of course we looked good going in with our hair and makeup on point. They served us plenty of red Jello shots. I can honestly say this bachelor really stayed in his place being very professional and nice to the girls. I made a killing off them. Stephanie was so sure Jerry wasn't into dark-skinned girls but he had sex with TooTall. I wonder what she had to say the next day?

But there was something special about being on campus. Katina would be introduced to, but not have sex with, players including George Goode, Terrence Jennings and Chris Smith. She regarded Smith as *"cool, quiet people."*

Don't talk much but gets the job done.

George Goode, jerk.

Terrence Jennings, laid back.

There was a reason Katina had stars in her eyes. She was seeing stars, or at least potential future stars.

Chris Smith was a senior starting guard for the Cardinals. Goode was a junior. Jennings would soon enter the NBA draft. Williams, known as T-Will, had been one of Pitino's superstars and had signed with the Houston Rockets. Behanan was a 6-7, 240-pound power forward with a bright future, but would be dismissed from the team later for repeated drug use. Goode, Jennings and Williams all were teammates of McGee during the 2008-2009 season. They occasionally showed up at dorm parties.

Katina had teamed up with a niece she called Boobie to help her with the arrangements.

Not only Boobie, the kids help out too. I don't know what I would do without them. They love Boobie to death. She makes all my phone calls and keeps the dancers together and notified. She goes to the shows with us, gets the girls

together, she collects the money, holds the money. Yeah, just
wait. Boobie, we gonna have it all, Mama.

Boobie confirmed that at the eight dorm parties she attended, they started with five or six players and recruits and before the evening ended there were 15 or more guys. She enjoyed Andre's likeable, funny personality.

On July 18, 2011, with Rod-Ni scheduled to soon join the federal Job Corps—she would be gone eight months or so and earn a certificate in the culinary arts—Katina reported:

Well, U of L is trying to have us put on a big show before
Rod-Ni leaves. Andre McGee wants us to do our sixth show for
U of L. McGee is crazy about Rod-Ni but she ain't crazy about
him! Sorry McGee. U cool and all. But you're just no-fuck

Rod-Ni and Chane Behanan in McGee's room in the dorm

material to everyone. Don't get it twisted though McGee is a long-winded nigga and can go for hours, but he's just McGee. The team should be leaving soon to go to the Bahamas to have 10 practice games. They probably be over there fucking these chicks and ain't no telling what they bring back. I'm glad that I am retired from dancing at U of L. Can't say the money ain't good but I have put my fair share in when I first did a show for Tink. Now I book them, get paid off top and we good.

The dancers I have now are cool. They basically know the drill and how I am. I'm always down to make cake. I expect $300 just to walk through the door. Now if it's a private show I charge $100 to walk in, then I start the bid: $$$$$.

One player all the women admired was Behanan. Powell wrote:

I need to get on the ball with Chane. Rod-Ni is gone and I need tickets to U of L games. It would be nice to sort of be in Chane's corner because the nigga's a star. I also get tickets from Andre McGee in exchange for private shows for the team and new recruits. He's mad because he couldn't fuck my daughter before she left to go to Job Corps.

She said McGee wasn't her type, plus he's annoying. But she really has a crush on Chane's sexy ass.

He's tall, light brown skinned, very respectful, but he's a basketball thug. This nigga cops weed, he loves weed, he says whatever the fuck he wants, and overall he's a beast on the court. Yes, I need front row seats to this. Every time we do a show you can always expect Mr. Chane to participate.

Not only was Rod-Ni gone temporarily, daughter Lindsay had enrolled in school and was trying to get a regular job. But Shay had expressed interest in joining the troupe. Katina wrote:

Shay, my baby, she is crazy but I love her. Now that Rod-Ni's gone she has been all up under me, which is good. Asshole, 'her sperm donor,' missed out on a lot of fun times with her. She's pretty, she's smart, she's a real joker. She's good though almost seventeen with a bang-in body. I'm glad that I did it by myself.

On August 5, 2011, there was another party for U of L.

Of course you know my nigga McGee set it all up for us. I really dig McGee 'cause he's cool, he treats us with the utmost respect. He jokes a lot but all in all he takes care of us. Of course you know Chane was there. So we took pictures, me and another cat and McGee. We did a show for a younger recruit. The girls took care of him. So he should choose U of L as his college. (We've) done so many recruits it's sickening.

I don't dance, so it's funny watching the other girls get their money. McGee asked me to go to Miami to do a bachelor party for his brother. I wanna go so bad and so do the other girls.

McGee, Katina and Russ Smith at a party in the dorm

On September 24, 2011, anticipation heightened because it was Behanan's birthday.

> *Everybody is going to want to go to that show, 'cause Chane's so cool, that everybody loves him. I'll probably dance in this one. Yeah, it's time to come out of retirement. Hope Rod-Ni comes home for this one. He would be happy to see her....*
>
> *We need several jerseys #21 with Behanan on the back. Booty shorts with black heels. Underneath we need to have on a red bra/black thongs. Bring him drinks. Feed him. Massage him. Give him one helluva show.*
>
> *All the girls like Chane. I already got them asking do I get Chane this time? Craziness. They just don't faze me that way. I think they're cool. It's funny to watch the girls when Chane walks in. He's a doll-baby!!*

The next day, Katina reported on a bonus from the show:

Rod-Ni and Peyton Siva in the dorm after a party.
Siva took pictures of the dancers but didn't have sex.

This time we got a chance to meet Peyton Siva. He came into the room sexy as can be. My dancers went nuts, Rod-Ni was back and had a chance to give him a no-sex massage. He was very sweet and polite. My dancers side-dealed (sex) with a couple of new recruits through me and Andre. I took Lindsay, TooTall, Precious, J.J. and Rod-Ni. It was in the basketball players' dorm. The girls were dressed to impress. Even campus security had to back up and take another look.

Siva was a sophomore guard on the Cardinals. He didn't have sex with the girls.

In late October, Katina Powell and McGee texted each other:

McGee: whats up with a show Saturday night?

Powell: U tell me. 4 who

McGee: This kid who already decided to come here but this will be his first time visiting

Powell: Ok that's cool. Give me details later

McGee: I'm telling you now cause we gotta talk about prices. I can't keep spitting out 200 to 250 up front. Its basketball season…so we got some tickets…so lets talk.

Powell: OK lets talk tickets then

McGee: 2 tickets to a game equals what?

Powell: $100 and two good tickets. No bullshit games. I got a lot of chicks that wanna go.

McGee: Aint no game a bullshit game!! Theres a game tma night. Then Saturday night…that sound cool?

Powell: A real game. No exhibition game. I don't know, we will see.

A few days later they had another show at the dorm.

Katina took Lindsay, TooTall, M.J. and Ne-Ne.

M.J, according to Katina, was especially popular because of a beautiful face and large behind. Ne-Ne was what Katina called a "gutter chick" who preferred sex to dancing and had four children of her own.

We had a new recruit from Cleveland named Terry, dark-skinned, big black dick. This time I copped out and took tickets instead of money. 2 sets of tickets. Rod-Ni is gonna be proud. Long Beach State and Ohio. This time it was TooTall and Ne-Ne that took down the new recruit, but I know that it was my girl TooTall that worked her magic. Get it, girl.

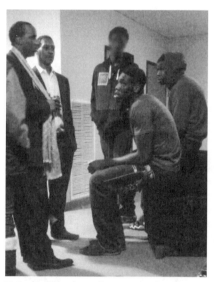

McGee (far left), unknown frequenter, recruit standing, Anton Gill (far sitting), Montrezl (front sitting) in the dorm before a party.

I think it's time we slow down for U of L. I wouldn't want McGee to get in trouble. He only means well. He spends his money on this shit, and, believe me, it's not cheap. He gives the guys money to throw at the girls. He constantly has to go to the ATM to get money out, $300 for me, $300 in tips for the girls, tickets for me. Alcohol for the recruits when they come, three bottles of Ciroc liquor, which is *about $30 a bottle. And this is at least twice a month.*

At this rate, by the time I'm done my girls will be basketball wives for sho.

For all of the ballyhoo and posturing, some things about the parties bothered Katina. She wrote:

(The ladies) having sex with the recruits had its ups and downs. Some of these guys were babies and didn't know the first thing about having sex, and for other recruits the girls said some of them knew how to work it off the court.

The biggest hype at U of L was who would cum first. Andre teased some of the guys about how fast they would cum and how he was wasting money on guys who took no time to cum.

Katina, Mangok Mathiang and Shay. Mathiang stopped by one of the parties in the men's dorm but didn't have sex.

28

The looks on these kids' faces was s ometimes heart-breaking, because it was all too much for them. Think about it. You are a senior in high school and you get the opportunity to have sex with these highly experienced females, and you don't want to say no because it makes you look soft in all areas, so you have to do it. I hand-picked these girls so they had the best of the best.

There were times when I would look at the recruit's face and they would look so lost, like this was not something they were expecting on their visit to U of L. A high school kid, some you could tell it was their first time sexually. Sometimes it would be one girl on a guy, sometimes two girls on a guy. It was whatever they wanted at that time to make them sign.

Andre always supplied the condoms for the guys.

At times there was the fear of being caught, by a recruit's family—by his mother, at least.

The scariest thing that I experienced at U of L was when two girls were in a room with a recruit and they had all gotten undressed ready to get started and his mom back-tracked and came back to the dorm for her son. Andre ran into the room and told him to hurry up and get dressed, his mom was out there. He told us to stay in the room and don't come out or make a sound.

Katina often serviced parents of recruits.

I only ever had sex with one recruit because I had enough girls to take care of that for me. I had sex with the parents because that's just the way it was set up. He (Andre) would call me and tell me that it was a parent of the recruit and I had to make him feel good enough to send his son to U of L.

All I knew was that it had to be done without questioning, so I never asked. I just did the job. And I was damn good at what I did. Andre would meet me at the hotel where the father was

29

staying, pay me, and take off before he was seen by anyone.

There were other escort clients to be serviced during this time, and some were even more risky than running into a recruit's mother. In November 2011 Katina did a party for the birthday of a police officer. She wrote:

I was kind of nervous because he called me before asking for a string of shows. I almost turned them down because I didn't know exactly how much I could trust them, let alone a cop. There was a pool table downstairs that the girls were dancing on.

The officer took her upstairs.

I got my money first though. We had sex on the twin bed. Once he got on top of me and starting changing positions, the bed broke and we both laughed. When he finished he put his head on my chest and started talking. The cop told me his whole life story, as if I cared. He said his wife is controlling, she has his phone tapped, he has to take care of his kids and his mom, on a cop's salary. Poor thang! Do I care? Hell no! I don't listen to any excuses that a nigga has, 'cause the bill collectors ain't listening to mine at all!!

I'M LIKE THE BANK OF LOUISVILLE.

-Katina Powell

While entertaining some of the University of Louisville's elite basketball players and providing sex to lure potential recruits proved to be a mainstay for Katina and her dancers, money also poured in from Katina's escort activities, some of them with her daughters.

She was already doing shows and the money was good, if not complicated. One firm for which she'd served as an escort took 60 percent of her earnings; she pocketed 40 percent.

She quit. But then money she made from bachelor parties and private shows started drying up.

> I struggled for a whole year straight. No shows, no bachelor parties. I begged and pleaded with God for a break. 'What can I do to make money?' Now, I'm no stranger to making money, but I was definitely a stranger to the infamous website Backpage.com.

The turning point came one day while she was sitting at home.

> My youngest daughter called and said, 'Mama, I'm making all this money. I went to St. Louis and posted on Backpage and made $1,000. I just bought me an iPad, brand new, new clothes, and everything. You should try it.' So basically everybody was eating off of the Backpage situation. Me, my other two daughters and (friend) TooTall was like, shit, okay, let's try it.
>
> So we go to my daughter's friend Lexi, a white girl who seems to be eating really good off this (Backpage), and she found us a picture to match our faces and different names of girls

out of town who had no desire to ever come to Louisville.
She posted me and my oldest daughter and 10 minutes later
everything changed for real...Now, I was used to escorting,
but this was totally different.

Katina took the name "Crystal, from Austin, Texas." She and her ladies got a room at Extended Stay. In the first day the phone rang 50 times, nonstop.

The game is that when one person has a call, the other person
leaves but don't go too far. There were three of us, so we
stayed moving. The second day we were all by ourselves
(no Lexi), but we made it work, scared, and all took calls from
guys, watched out for one another.

I'll never forget, I had this one big muscle-bound guy who
Lindsay didn't want so she passed him to me. All he kept
asking was why are you doing this, I can take you away
from all this. I told him you called me, so if you didn't call I
wouldn't be doing this. It got to the point where I was posting
every day. One day alone I made almost $1,000 on everything.

Business was booming. Besides Katina it now involved several other women including Lindsay, TooTall, Rod-Ni, Lexi, Shay, Loren and Hannah.

I was probably the only one doing it with her kids. We booked
room after room: Galt House, Red Roof, Extended Stay, the
Hyatt, the Sheraton. Red Roof was Number 1. Men came from
all over, Louisville, Indiana, Fort Knox, Lexington and all the
surrounding areas. Our names were Crystal, Ashley, Sammi,
Lexi, Desiree and Queen.

At this rate they almost needed more than one room.

The crazy thing about it is that our calls would conflict with
the other person's, four people to a room and everybody's

phone is going off. So we're overbooking people, now the next person wouldn't get to take an in-call. In-call means you get a spot or a room and they come to you. Out-call means they tell you where they are at and you go to them.

But as business grew so did Katina's worries. They could have been robbed. Or a man might crave more than what she was offering.

If you offer more, you take a chance of getting an STD (sexually transmitted disease). You never know when a female has gotten his phone and decided to contact you for your number being in her mate's phone. Men could stalk you or make a personal scene in public or when you're with your mate. All sorts of things. But I think the scariest is getting busted by law enforcement or getting sick and not knowing what's really wrong.

I got really sick one day. Now I work for Genevieve Cleaning Company that requires me to clean up after college kids on the U of L campus; bathrooms, kitchens, bedrooms. Now, mind you these are college kids who don't give a fuck one way or the other. By not covering up my face and the nails breaking through my latex gloves I'm assuming that some sort of bacteria got into my system.

At the same time, a few calls gave me a huge scare that continues to scare me to this day. There was a few guys that slipped out of the condom. One guy came and when he did the protection filled up with blood—the scariest thing of my life. But nothing got on or in me. I panicked. I instantly thought, what if I have something? What if it touched me? I had diarrhea for four weeks. I got tested for STDs; negative. I had nothing but that wasn't satisfying to me 'cause the big test is what matters.

At one point she tried to design a male condom that couldn't come off accidentally.

Katina's business activities weren't exactly secret. She would also become a tireless promoter of her business. There were cards, brochures, advertisements, radio blurbs, word of mouth, always in pursuit of one goal—money and more money.

Katina dreamed up special shows featuring seductive scenes and role-playing. Her money-making ideas included an office and home-cleaning service featuring sexy women. Here are more:

NAMES FOR THE NEW SHOW!!

Sex Toyz and Playboyz

Dancers Cum To Life

Platinum's Secrets

A Touch of Gold

Cum take a swirl with the hottest play girls.

A hypnotic party—when you come, give me some

A French Lick on the biggest dick

Baskets for the females. Cages for the girls. Peep shows. A female with tricks behind the curtains. When shows over cover her up.

Each guy gets 2 minutes behind the Curtains.

She must be able to perform many (variety) of tricks.

In late 2011, she wrote:

People, it's almost time for my third show, and I am so nervous. I took a chance and bet on this new club called T-9. It's a very spacious club with a lot of rooms, three big rooms and a small room. U of L is supposed to be there. So the pressure is on. I have to set up V.I.P. for them.

Ticket to Club T-Nine show which McGee attended

I have to have two servers, two massagers, six dancers, one headliner, one human buffet, girls on the pool table.

Girls on the pool table have to play around while they shoot pool naked.

As it turned out, the show at Club T-Nine proved to be a hit.

Photo shoot before the show at Club T-Nine

I'm not gonna lie, I didn't think a whole lot of people was gonna be there. It was almost packed.

I had 12 beautiful females that were new faces.

I had a human buffet that was truly gorgeous.

I had a private room with red-light specials going on. I had chicks on the pool table playing pool nude. And to top it off, I had the most beautiful massage room, with an all-white massage table, see-through curtains, and red lights that really enhanced the room.

Grateful for success, Katina wrote a kind of poem prayer:

Dear God, for those who know

I take tremendous pride when doing a show.

A lot of people think that I'm a ho

And these people know exactly where to go.

I do my best to keep it under wrath

Will step on anything and anyone who gets in my path.

Her entrepreneurial mind was always churning with new ideas. She confided in her diary:

I just sit and think about all kinds of shit. Like a sex play that would be clean, like some kind of skit. Yeah, that would be hot. Anything with more appeal to it. Have a few actors and actresses on board. Props like couches, beds, tables, all kinds of sexual props. Do tricks and pole tricks for other women to see. Put on the play for about 20 or 30 minutes. Special effects and outfits. Toys, massage tables, all kinds of shit.

You could set it up like a hotel. Let a man walk in the room to two females playing with one another. Soft music, almost everything

Human buffet

38

without straight fucking. 2 percent to the imagination. Get some gay shit to play the female on female skit.

Katina knew her customers, though with a cynical view of her key demographic.

I know that 99% of all men cheat. Since I've been in this industry it has been proven time and again, married men who claim that they have no interest in their mates at all. Some would call back-to-back claiming that they need a behind the scenes girlfriend that loves to kiss and is always available. The whole damned world is to me corrupt. No morals or values anywhere because people feel that it's just sex and everybody is doing it. Crazy because the boyfriend and I always argue about morals and values when it comes to struggling. Some people do it for the struggle and some people do it for the sport. Such an addiction when it comes to escorting.

I guess you can say that escorting is a job 'cause you make your own prices and hours. I am the CEO. People call you all hours of the night. When you first post and put your pic at the top (well, your ad) the phone rings nonstop. Since doing this, including shows, my name has changed several times. I have been SinAmen, Platinum, Crystal, Roxy Ray, Kream, too many to remember. This industry is no more than acting.

*You're selling them their fantasy. You can be who you want.
I was in character for Crystal. I was 29, from Austin, Texas,
thick, curvy, and loved to party and make money. Kream was
more outgoing, cared (but I didn't really care) about your day,
your job and your problems. There were times that clients
would be talking to me and my mind would be elsewhere
thinking about what me and my boyfriend could do.*

*Oh, yes, I have a boyfriend, but, see, this is where I'm at with
it: I love my boyfriend unconditionally and I never confuse the
two at all. I love my man with all my heart. I wanna spoil him,
give him the best. I want us to see things that he wouldn't
think of seeing. I want us to explore the world together.*

*Yeah, I've made pretty good money doing this. Have I sold
my soul? I don't feel as though I have but some people beg to
differ. But okay, in one night I made a lot of money.*

The money allowed me to do a lot of what I wanted to do.

The money generated from Katina's erotic empire had a funny
way of soothing uneasiness some family and friends might have had
about it.

*Everyone in my family knew and still knows about what's
going on. My father, my sisters, of course my brothers, the
kids (my proud supporters), and of course whether he wants
to admit it or not, my boyfriend. I think they all support me
because they need money at any given time. I'm like the Bank
of Louisville. What trips me out is that if anyone has a big
problem with what I do, I don't know it. Would I stop if my
family told me to? U answer that question!!*

At times Katina reflected on her profession:

*Sex sells! It's one of the highest-paying industries. I think it's
more exotic to men when they pay for it. It gives them a sense*

of power. They can be whoever they wanna be at the moment. You would be amazed at what people will ask you to do, where they ask you to go. The shit gets serious. They pay for threesomes, late nights. I've never been with a female doing this. I've had plenty of men inquire about their female friends.

A man asked if he could be 13 and I be his mom and he got into trouble in school. If I would discipline him while I was naked. (Pervert). Shows that he was thinking about his mother.

Is escorting different from prostitution? My definition of an escort is a very classy professional woman that can turn it on at the drop of a dime. A male or female that can keep him coming to his liking. An escort sets her price up front.

She's invited to the suites in some of the most luxurious hotels in or out of town. Travels to do her job and does it very discreetly.

Prostitute's an outdated term. Women that really don't care, that don't have to turn it up. A woman that walks up and down the street until she's chosen, not caring who may see 'cause she wants everybody to see her. A prostitute doesn't have an amount 'cause anything will do. But I think it's the same. Hell, yeah, you're still selling something.

Just a classier, newer title but the same business.

People come to see me because they know what I can give:
1. I'm bigger than the club scene. Strip clubs had a few customers, but my shows were packed to capacity.
2. I'm gonna give you what you can't get at home. Girlfriends and wives don't give head and don't like to ride.
3. I give you up to 98% of your imaginations.

Katina understands the special risks inherent in her business:

Almost getting robbed, it was the scariest shit ever. For real this one nigga (yes, nigga) with his ratchet ass called me and asked me to come and do an outcall at his apartment. His story was that he needed a female to come to his place because he was paralyzed, or had been shot. He said he had been robbed so he needed me to come by myself. He said the last person he trusted robbed and shot him. He said he had $800 for two hours.

I thought it was too good to be true, but my dumb ass goes anyway. I took Lindsay with me. So we get there and he's already fidgety, looking around. I'm looking for the quickest way out. Then he goes to the couch and starts looking under it. He goes to the table and pulls out a glove, puts it on, goes back to the couch, lifts it up further, then says, 'I'm not gonna shoot y'all. I'm just looking for the gun.'

What the fuck kind of shit is that? Whoever was supposed to

leave the gun in a certain spot under the couch must have moved it 'cause his dumb ass couldn't find it. We got out of there.

There are other, peculiar perils in Katina's business:

One morning, I received a phone call from a known number.

At first I didn't recognize it 'cause it was like 6 a.m. So he's like, 'yeah, can you do an out-call?' I'm like 'to where?'

Katina's dancers at a Louisville Club

He said 'the west end (of Louisville)'. So the more he talked the more I caught on to his voice. I looked in the phone to see the number. I'm like 'whereabouts in the west end do you live? 'When he told me, it's like, 'oh, shit'. I told him I'd call him back. So I texted him it was going to be $100 for an hour, He said all I got is $85. I'm like, nothing less than $100.

So he said OK, just come on. I asked him what was the exact address. When he told me I could have passed out because it was my boyfriend and my address!

It was my stepson.

I THINK OTHER PEOPLE KNEW,
BECAUSE WE DID THIS FOR ALMOST FOUR YEARS.
WHITE GUYS WALKED THE HALLS;
IT HAD TO GET TO (OTHER COACHES).

-Katina Powell

The early months of 2012 began with the prospects of a good year for Katina Powell and company as U of L's unofficial recruiting team.

Katina's sometimes-strained relationship with McGee relaxed a bit. She began to regard him as a friend, not just as a customer.

On February 13, 2012, Katina scribbled in her diary:

> *Andre McGee from U of L called and asked me if I was interested in making some big money. He had a coach who invited some out of town guys to the U of L-Syracuse game.*
>
> *Of course you know I'm interested, it's money. There were two of them, Dejuan and T.K. aka Travis, Hyatt Regency.*
>
> *$300 and all tips. Of course there was sexual intercourse with the guys and two dancers. Total of five girls in the room.*

McGee was to meet Katina in the Hyatt parking lot to pay her. He arrived early and went to a bar for a drink. When Katina showed up, she took a picture of his car and license plate and the girls laughed as she proclaimed, *"He can't say we weren't here."*

She wrote later:

> *The guys were well pleased, except for one lil' situation when they said one of the dancers had an odor. That threw me for a loop. I didn't smell anything at all, but they seem to wanna say that they smelled her off the muscle. I have to thank McGee for the hookup.*
>
> *They said they were gonna invite us down to Memphis to do a*

McGee's car in the parking lot of the Hyatt   *License plate of McGee's car*

show in April for some frat brothers. I'm in. I need money in
hand before I do anything. They even asked us was we going
to the All-Star Game. It would be nice, but I doubt it.

Again in March, a similar entry:

Did a private show for U of L. Some new recruits, as usual.
I took Lindsay, Rod-Ni, TooTall and M.J. Chane Behanan, who
is a beast in basketball, came in the room for a second....
This time I allowed McGee to pay me $200 and tips. A couple
of days later he turned me on to two dudes from Tennessee
and Florida who went to the Louisville game. It was at the
Hyatt Regency. They paid $200.

Katina admired McGee's commitment to improving U of L's
talent. She wrote later:

Andre and I had an amazing relationship for the most part of
our journey. He was an amazing person. He stopped at no cost
to make sure that U of L had the best recruits from all over.
The dancers took him a different way than I did. They thought
occasionally he was funny, but very cocky and arrogant.
He always had jokes for the dancers. Some laughed and some
didn't crack a smile.
Andre and I always had the agreement that he could never have
the girls' numbers personally or contact the girls without me. A few
times he tried to go behind my back, and I blooped out. He told me

46

to calm down and he would never do it again, and he never did.

McGee, she said, often came across as cocky and confident, but she sensed that *"deep down he was under a lot of pressure from the coaches. He always said his job depended on this kid signing."* Katina believed that McGee was, if nothing else, loyal to his coach, saying, *"you could look into his eyes and see the loyalty he had for Pitino. To him he was just doing his job."*

Some things were peculiar to her, however. While McGee always liked to say that the ATM was his best friend, many times his cash was wrapped in bank bands—stacks of money with white bands around it and nothing you could get from an ATM.

> *I never questioned exactly where the money came from,*
> *I just knew he had help because his account couldn't handle*
> *expenses alone.*
>
> *Andre would stand on the couch and throw money. He'd give*
> *it to the guys to throw. It was loud. He'd say, 'Shit's getting*
> *sloppy. Don't come in those clothes!'*

Over time, the earlier secrecy had completely evaporated.

For their appearances at the dorm, the women came to the front door and McGee let them in.

> *I think other people knew, because we did this for almost*
> *four years. White guys walked the halls; it had to get to (other*
> *coaches). Alumni players would come back and make Andre feel*
> *like crap. Andre sat at the end of the bench and looked miserable.*

They would ridicule him because he hadn't achieved as much as they had.

On April 30, 2012, Pitino promoted McGee to director of basketball operations.

"We're excited to have Andre continue with us in his new role," Pitino said in the announcement. "He's been learning for the last two years and has been extremely loyal to our program. He knows everything we do inside and out. I'm excited he is getting a break to move toward the coaching ranks."

According to the athletic department, the director of basketball operations reported to the head coach.

In mid-May, there was another show at the dormitory that was just for McGee himself, where McGee paid Katina $250. When she and the dancers arrived a girl was already there sitting on the couch with McGee.

> *Did a show for McGee and a biracial chick.*
>
> *This was a different kind of show. He was the only guy. I took TooTall, Margarette a new chick named Coco, Rod-Ni and myself. This mixed chick was drunk and so was McGee.*
>
> *One of my girls was giving the chick a lap dance. Another dancer was standing with her privates in the chick's face.*
>
> *The other two dancers were entertaining McGee. I've never seen a chick squirt and drip like her. Then to top it off McGee did something that totally shocked us. He played with this chick sexually in front of all of us. I don't think that we will ever forget this show.*

But McGee was worked up about other things as well. On June 1, as Katina was preparing for a $300 show that night for a recruit, she noted that McGee seemed to be under an inordinate amount of pressure:

> *McGee said he needs all the dancers to be on their A game, meaning he needs the girls to be down for after the show.*
>
> *He says that his job depends on it. His job is on the line.*
>
> *He says we really need this recruit.*

She added,

> *We usually get them to commit. The dancers I have going: TooTall, Ne-Ne, Coco, T-Mama, M.J. and Rod-Ni.*

Her report followed:

> *Did the show for U of L. Two new recruits, Jordan — from Dallas*

*and Montrezl from North Carolina.... Both recruits were taken
care of by two dancers. My job was to get them to sign to
Louisville by any means. $160, $80 apiece. Everybody was drunk.
McGee took care of everything. Yes, the new recruits (a 17-year-
old) were drinking Grey Goose.*

Montrezl Harrell was a 6-8 power forward who committed to
Louisville three days after the party.

That wasn't all.

*McGee needs a favor. The father of Jordan, from Dallas, Texas,
wanted a private show. McGee met me in the parking lot of the
SpringHill Suites in his new black shiny car he just bought two
weeks ago. He paid the $200 for both dancers. Then he pulled
off. The father of the player is a private investor. He flips houses.
He has a son in the NBA and another son in the NFL. He said he
loves Louisville, he loves our Yum Center, and Pitino is cool also.
(Most of the Cardinals' home games were played at the KFC Yum
Center in downtown Louisville.) That Coach Mike set it up for him.
I keep hearing about Coach Mike, he has set this up several times.
He's behind the scenes. But he's definitely active in these parties.
Thanks, Coach Mike.*

At the time, Louisville did not have a coach with that name.
Katina had never met the man and had made no further attempt to
identify him.

*But I really have a strange bond with McGee. That's my nigga
4 Real. He has spent well over $5,000, $6,000, if not more,
with me.*

*Chane Behanan wants to know about how much for a
threesome. He wanted Rod-Ni and me together, but we knew
that would never happen. He says he has $1,500.*

On and on it went. In mid-2012, Katina noted:

T-Will came to town and wanted two girls for his pleasure ($1,000). I took Rod-Ni, Tiara and Strawberry. He wanted Rod-Ni off the muscle. We met at McGee's new condo, under the viaduct by U of L. T-Will's girl was at a hotel. Once it was done, he was out. McGee took Tiara to the dorm. No money was exchanged by McGee.

Two days later:

Tiara in Billy Minardi Hall

Hotel SpringHill Suites. Money ($120) paid by McGee for a father of a student. Father's name is Jazzy from Dallas. (Katina slept with him.)

Katina ran into Chane Behanan.

He told me that he (and his friend Kenny) needs some females for a video. We can do that. Of course I don't wanna be in it. I just want that paper and exposure.

But later that June, Katina received a telephone call from McGee that would mark a turning point of sorts. He told her that the other coaches said they needed white girls, "clean white girls, that are down to fuck."

Rhythm-less, white-as-snow white girls, as she once described contemptuously a duo that worked for her. The demands for this season put strain on the McGee relationship:

> *I clocked out. Nigga, your demands ain't shit to me, but since we're speaking of demands it's time for me to raise my prices from $300 to $400 or $500. I don't even know who these people are with their demands. You know it's hard as hell to get white girls, let alone white girls that's down to fuck, that's a helluva ticket that those muthafuckas can't pay for AT ALL!!*

Katina prided herself in providing a variety of good talent, and tried to bring in new faces when she could during the three years she'd worked with him.

> *Now all of a sudden these pussy-ass redneck bastards got demands. I don't know where I'm gonna get white girls from. But I can do it. It's not impossible.*

The allusion to other coaches and the reference to white women angered Katina. She wrote:

> *I promise I'm waiting on the right time to take these bastards down. I have made thousands off these niggas and plan on making more. I had a lot of offers to do more strip parties with McGee, taking trips to other cities to service guys he knew. It was getting cloudy, though. I just have to be smart and patient as well. At the right time, when I decide to tell my story, I will tell my story.*

By that, Powell said she was not trying to set up the team for a fall. *"It wasn't to get anything out of anybody,"* she'd say, later. Rather, if someone tried coming back at her she would have evidence to show that services were requested from within U of L.

Katina had hurt feelings because of all she and her girls had done for McGee and the team. Now black women weren't sufficient for some of these clients, and some parents of recruits wanted private shows at their hotel rooms. McGee told her that the reason the team was getting so many recruits was "the love that they show them."

He said these guys could care less about the city or the school,
they care about seeing ass and tits at 17 and 18 years old.
So basically I'm the one bringing them and keeping them here.

Katina felt pressured to come up with white women to dance at the show, scheduled for September 7. She unloaded her frustration on her sister, Debbie.

I was telling her that I had an idea as far as what I've been
doing for U of L. I know I am only a small person when it
comes to big people and millions of dollars. But wrong is
wrong. I don't think that what I'm doing and what they
are doing is wrong in my eyesight. It's just business in the
industry. But to the legal people we're all in trouble.
People look at this as embezzlement, extortion and greed,
but people with no money looks at this as a straight come up.
If it was me that was being wrong, they would be after my
ass. All over the news, the newspaper, and most of all Crime
Time. *Don't want that shit.*
I'm not in the least bit scared. I'm cautious. I'm just gonna
chill and wait for the right time to explode. Why are people so
afraid of reality, and people with authority they can fall just
as hard as we can. I just wonder what would happen if I was
to open my mouth...
A lot of people don't want any part of any sort of sacrifice.
She said that they have the power to have something done to my

children. God, only God can have that done. I don't fear too easily.
I'm gonna give it a little more thought and a lot more evidence.

As she did occasionally. Katina prayed for divine help.

God, please give me the energy and the strength to get there.
To get back on track mind, body and spirit. Lord, please
allow me to recruit the right team of girls for this, at least
all through September. I have a million ideas but only a few
dollars to get started.

The next time McGee telephoned, in early September, her attitude had hardened. She wrote:

I've been dealing with McGee for three nearly years now.
He can pretty much tell in my voice that I'm getting impatient
with his bullshit. These niggas wanna demand some bullshit...
he asked me why has my attitude changed? I'm like, nigga,
when I was dealing with just you, it was cool. Now you got
these broke ass bootleg muthafuckas calling shots.
Hell, yeah, I got an attitude. First of all me and McGee don't
fuck around or side-deal at all, for that matter.

Katina was disgusted. McGee, she said, put a man on the phone who initially asked for a white girl. Then he changed his mind—asking for a "thick light-skinned female."

"Confused bastard," she scribbled in her diary.

He said that his buddies from the Hyatt Regency show we did
a while back told him that my dancer M.J. smelled. OK, he's
not lying about that. So for his demands I asked for $600. He
said she'd better do mad tricks for the $600.
It's to the point where I am about to say to hell with McGee,
the players, the coaches, just U of L period. I can't wait to get
there and snap pics of everything. When it's not at U of L, I
can't take pics. All I can do is document everything in my book

and pray that if shit hits the fan that my book will save me
and prove that illegal shit is truly on them.

Later, McGee, she added, offered $400 for one woman to be sent to the SpringHill Suites to have sex with an unidentified parent of one of the players. Katina considered sending Rod-Ni, but it didn't happen.

The next show at the dormitory was on September 8.

Besides regulars TooTall, Rod-Ni, Shay and T-Mama, she had two white dancers, Hannah and Loren.

> *who have entirely NO rhythm, white as snow. Oh my*
> *goodness, what am I going to do?*
> *Two recruits, two dark-skinned freshmen. (One) with glasses*
> *who looks like he's from Africa. There was (another) with*
> *braids, a light-skinned guy whose job is holding down the*
> *dorm. The ones who side-dealed (arranged by McGee and I)*
> *were TooTall and T-Mama, $80 apiece. I sent the white girls*
> *away. I don't want them to get scared or go and run their*
> *mouths. I did something I don't normally do, and that is let*
> *McGee pay me later.*

The next day, she wrote, McGee texted her and said he would pay her the following day. It was two days later, however, when Katina wrote, McGee paid her $300 for the dancers.

> *McGee wanted some pussy, but he knows he can't get it from*
> *me. I met him at his apartment (the Reynolds Lofts condo on*
> *campus). He told me the guy with the braids stole a cell phone*
> *and some Jordans (3 pair).*

In mid-September, McGee was on the phone again.

> *Got a call from McGee asking me do I have two females that's*
> *down to fuck. Of course you know I'm gonna use T-Mama and*
> *TooTall. We're supposed to meet at the Boys Dorm. I'm curious*
> *to know what recruit this one is.*

A men's basketball dorm room

Anyway, McGee for some reason seems to wanna keep paying me later. I keep saying that I'm gonna quit fooling with this fool. McGee wanted to have a slumber party with me and the dancers just to kick it with him. $200 for dancers, $150 for me =$350. That never happened.

With three of her dancers, Katina met McGee at the dormitory and they went to the Hyatt Regency to meet a friend of McGee's who had a twelfth-floor room. Katina didn't meet the man.

The girls said he was fat, lame and wack.

As I always say, you gotta take the good with the bad when it comes to money. I feel sorry for McGee because he wanted to be taken care of, by all the girls, but everybody knows that McGee takes 4Eva and a day to cum. Even T-Mama don't want to fuck with him.

Change was in the wind. Later, Katina wrote:

It's game time, folks!! Yeah, buddy U of L is back to their bullshit. I heard that McGee ain't gonna give us tickets this season. That's cool. No tickets, no pussy from dancers.

Can U deal with that, muthafucka?

MOMMY, I DON'T THINK OF US AS PROSTITUTES.
I JUST THINK WE DID IT FOR THE FUN.

-Rod-Ni

Periodically, when there were no invitations to dance at the University of Louisville men's dormitory and other types of parties and encounters were few and far between, Katina wrote of personal problems and family matters. Or, as might be expected, family problems.

Her narcissism and self-confidence, sometimes shaken, returned in diary entries like this one:

> *This nigga is talking about eating my pussy until I come*
> *numerous times. If I went into a relationship I would give him*
> *a run for his money. I haven't even touched this nigga and*
> *he's already sprung.*
>
> *Life is amazing. I am truly the pick of the litter. I am doing*
> *my best to keep these niggas off me. It's hard but nice to be*
> *thought of and admired by niggas and bitches!!*

In contrast:

> *This weed thing is killing me 4 sure. I really need to stop*
> *smoking. I buy weed like every day, it seems like that's where*
> *all my money goes. I could probably be a millionaire if I just*
> *stop smoking. I think niggas have me on speed dial when they*
> *get it in. Truth! I'm paying niggas car payments/furniture bills/*
> *food expenses. For real! I know I spend at least $200 a week.*
> *That's fucked up!*

Nevertheless, she admitted in one entry:

Yeah, maybe I'm crazy, but I let Shay smoke on Christmas.

I know, I know, but she's always treated so differently.

And did we honestly think that with all of us smoking that she wouldn't be the least bit interested? I feel a little bad because I don't want her to form a habit. We do it and expect our kids not to do it. Wrong message.

I know my child. She's a bit confused right now but she will get through this phase and develop into a beautiful, confident young woman. With a job.

Not much later, this admission:

I smoke weed and blacks (thin cigars). So does Lindsay, Rod-Ni, and Shay. I feel sort of bad that all of us smoke, but, worse than that, they are broke and can't afford the damn habit. So who do they come to? ME! Like now that we discovered Shay smokes, she's constantly on my ass about give me some weed, let me hit your black.

In January 2012, Katina wrote of Shay's birthday:

Today is my Baby's Birthday! Happy birthday, I love you so much. Even though you get on my nerves you're still my lil' Princess. Have a wonderful birthday, ur 17 now, almost grown. I LOVE YOU BABE!!

To her relief, Shay, like Rod-Ni before her, eventually signed up for the federal Job Corps as a way to complete her GED faster. (Rod-Ni could at least self-identify with another role in life, telling her mother at one point: "Mommy, I don't think of us as prostitutes. I just think we did it for fun."). Katina wrote:

I really miss Shay! She called me (from the Job Corps) the other night, crying. I hate for my kids to be anywhere unhappy. I just want her to get her diploma. I don't want my selfishness to hurt her. I miss hearing her voice, seeing her beautiful face. I love my kids so much, they are truly my best friends.

In May of that year, the family learned that Lindsay was pregnant and would have her baby in December 2012.

I'm so excited about my grandbaby.

Meanwhile, she was scratching out ideas for her next show at Club T-Nine, with the theme "Illusions of Porn." She wrote:

Private room, massage room, pool table, human buffet, drinking human buffet, pole dancing competition between two girls, girl with most money wins. Five dancers, total. Need one male dancer. Illusions of Porn: everything done with a sheet. All the sexual acts and scenes will be covered up.

A bar scene between him and her. Everything but the real deal. Need the microphone for sound proof.

She worried about getting enough dates for her dance troupe.

All these females that do shows for me really look to me for work, and I be feeling bad when nothing comes up. Shit has really been slow and hopefully it will pick up, 'cause Lord knows I need that cash. I was thinking as many shows that I do, I hated the strip club, it's not a money spot, but you can't take your clothes off, and that's up my alley. I just need a couple of good solid workouts, and the kid is back.

Perhaps that accounted for a new entry:

I went to church today. I needed it. The topic was WELL DONE. The pastor is a beast with preaching. I wish I could go every day. He's the truth. He said that when you look upon and wish you had what other people got, your blessings come to a halt. God gives us our blessings, not other people. We got what we got due to the faithfulness and determination of God.

However, she took a part-time job at a cleaning service. Among other things, she needed money to buy marijuana. She wrote:

You guys, I want to take the next step in life. I wanna admit to my faults. Guy told me I should try a meeting, a W.A. meeting, Weed Anonymous or whatever you want to call it. I do have a problem, but I'm scared my sobriety of weed will cause me to pick up another addiction.

But really, I do need to go to a few classes, anything to get my life on track. I'm honestly scared, because maybe I'm fighting responsibilities of the real world. Shit, I don't know. What I do know is that I really, really, really love weed.

I can say that at this point. I'm glad and truly blessed that it's not a stronger drug like crack and other shit. My friend Crazy Joe has been clean now for seven years. Wow! That's a long time to be free of drugs. All I need is a pound of that good-good Dro (marijuana). And I would be perfectly fine.

Two months later, she had new employment with a damage restoration firm.

I got a new job, at Rosie's Restoration, with Shay, my partner in crime. I really love working with Shay 'cause she's cool.

But this guy named Shannon is my boss and this fat muthafucka asked could he pay for a little kissing (ha).

Not that he's fat as hell. But check this out, his paycheck for two weeks was $2,300 (like damn, he can afford to pay me for kissing). He gets on Shay's nerve, that's what's so funny.

Meanwhile, the need to have major dental surgery because of a car accident with an 18-wheeler truck, jolted her. Her mouth hit the steering wheel which resulted in all of her teeth having to be re-done.

On October 24, 2012, she wrote:

It seems like my whole life, image and personal life has changed. Of course everybody knows how I feel about my appearance. Yesterday made it no better. I've been asking

*myself and God, why me? What have I done to have this
stressing me out so bad? The dentist said that basically there
is nothing he can do except immediate surgery. So I'm gonna
be out of commission for about two to three weeks. I can't
talk to anyone or go around anyone for a long time. I cried in
the dentist's office, I cried in the car, I cried at home.*

Two weeks later, there were other things to cry about: her
brother.

*Last night me, Rod-Ni and Shay were watching the TV show
'Lockup Louisville—Extended Stay.' Guess who the damn
episode was about? Goddamn, Deshawn, 'Rock.' He was in for
armed robbery of a dice game. I feel so sorry for him at times.
These niggas act hard in the streets but when it's time to
throw 'em these niggas nut up like 'lil boyz. I know my daddy
is trippin' 'cause he spends all his money on Rock's lawyer,
and Rock is still acting a fool. He's enjoying the fact that he's
on TV and niggas are scared of him.*

To make matters worse, Rock had also recently crashed a moped
into a fire hydrant and was seriously injured. About a month later he'd
been shot eight times after straying into a dangerous housing project.

*But what people don't understand is that the scariest nigga is
the most dangerous muthafucka. The craziest thing about this
is that my brother got skillz. He can rap his ass off.*

*Plus the nigga is one helluva leader. He can get the whole
world to follow him if he wanted it that way. I know that deep
down in his heart he wants to do better. He only listens to
certain people, though.*

*God, please place your hands on Rock. Guide him your way
and place him on the right track. Lead him down the right
path. Give him wisdom and knowledge to know right from*

wrong. Allow him to think B-4 reacting. Allow him to look
forward to life, a new life and a new beginning. Place love in
his heart and freedom in his hands, God.

Taking stock in November, Katina found little to cheer about.
As she wrote, she was turning 40, "not so cool." Her truck had
broken down and would cost $300 to repair. She had lost her job.

I think the thing that hurts me the most is my mouth. No one
can really understand what I'm going through. I know that a
lot of things come in time and with age, but I never would have
imagined that my teeth would have to be pulled. I have to gain my
secureness back. It may take a while, but I'm a try to do it.

Right after that, she discovered that some 700 text messages
with McGee had disappeared from her phone because of a virus.
She wanted to write a book, and she was angry. She had copied
some of them down, and later would retrieve many of them, but the
episode "taught me a valuable lesson, to stop procrastinating and do
stuff right away."

On December 5, she wrote:

I can't wait for things to get better. Don't get me wrong or seem
as though I'm always complaining, but, DAMN, I've been so down
and depressed that it's taking control of my everyday life. This shit
just got so real.

Like not only do I need a job, I need a new hustle. I'm not scared
of competition, I'm just not in the game like I used to, but it's
crazy because people keep asking me to do shows. All my old
people been calling. My cousin Gregory keeps asking, because he
would rather go to one of my shows than a strip club. My niece
keeps saying we need to break bread (make money).

I really need to get motivated again. But what can get me
motivated?

Finally, things brightened a little.

Of course you guys know that our favorite team is back in season, U of L basketball team, my niggas and white boyz!! The season just started so they haven't called in a minute, 'cause they're going hard on the practices. They look pretty good on the court with their new uniforms with wings and their new attitudes.

Russ is my nigga—he's so sweet and polite with his white boy swagger. Blackshear with his bedroom eyes. He's a freak though, he wants threesomes on a regular. (Like Chane, Blackshear always asked but never had the money to do it.)

Russ Smith and Wayne Blackshear were guards. Both came to parties frequently, she said.

Chane Behanan from what I'm hearing is in a little bit of trouble, he can't do interviews or talk to the press. I saw Chane in the summer when I was working in the cleaning business. He was off the chain so when we went to the apartment that he was in it smelled like straight Ono (major weed).

Behanan eventually was suspended and later dismissed from the team for chronic drug use.

Old themes came back to the diary:

This weed thing has really got to stop. I'm like sick that no one has weed in the east end. I need to start recording how much weed I smoke in a week's time, 4Real.

I talk to God so much that I know I'm getting on his nerves. I feel bad for constantly asking when I should be grateful for what I have and the fact that I could be in worse situations.

I know that God's work is never done. God, I need you. I need guidance. I'm giving up on myself and I don't wanna do that. I just want my mind to be free. Right now my head is really cloudy.

On December 26, Lindsay delivered a healthy boy, nicknamed D.A., and Katina wrote:

> *I got to witness the whole birth. He is more than I expected, he's light-skinned, dark gray eyes and very good hair. I'm so proud of Lindsay for having such a beautiful child. She seems to be happier now that she has someone to call her own.*
>
> *I can't, we can't stop loving on him. We are so grateful that God blessed us with him.*

MCGEE CALLED AND ASKED IF I COULD BRING TWO
FEMALES UP TO U OF L TO 'TAKE CARE OF' TWO NEW
RECRUITS AND A PARENT WHO IS VISITING.
LATER HE CALLED AND SAID HE NEEDED A WHOLE
SHOW. I'M LIKE, NIGGA, MAKE UP YOUR DAMN MIND.

-Katina Powell

The approach of the new year, 2013, began with a promising harbinger from Andre McGee.

On December 29, 2012, Katina wrote:

> *Got a text message from McGee. He said they needed a show.*
> *If they win they need a big show, if they lose they want a*
> *small show. Well, they actually beat Kentucky, first time in*
> *four years, so they were pumped. I took T-Mama, her friend*
> *Ne-Ne, TooTall and Rod-Ni.*

McGee wanted the girls to dress normally when they arrived at the dorm to get past security. So the girls quit wearing high heels and wore T-shirts and shorts and then changed into their dance outfits in the dorm bathroom.

Dancer in the basketball dorm bathroom

We got there about 11:15 p.m. at the dorm. We took pics with McGee, Siva, Behanan, a recruit, a tall dark-skinned guy and another guy whose face I will never forget. I was shocked that Siva stayed as long as he did. Chane always fucks with us with his pill poppin' ass. The one dude that was there when I use to do it with Honey and Meka (Honey and I fucked him) but yeah that nigga was there trying to cop some weed. McGee paid me $600 cash for T- to fuck the one guy whose name I have yet to get. TooTall fucked the new recruit. Rod-Ni fucked the tall dark guy (Montrezl Harrell) *who's always joking on how fast a nigga cums.*

Once again that left McGee who knew that for the right money we could have got it poppin (just kidding) He tried but he wouldn't be McGee if he didn't. That's my nigga for real. I have to come up with a way for both of us to make some money before I write my tell-all book.

Montrezl Harrell and Rod-Ni before a show at the dorm

In late winter, with the NCAA tournament approaching and the Cardinals figuring to be a strong contender, anticipation grew, but Katina's focus was on domestic matters.

In early March she wrote:

> *It's three o'clock in the morning and I can't sleep. I must have gone to bed pretty early. As they say on Facebook, it's wake and bake time (time to smoke).*
>
> *I'm so proud of the girls (the kids) for trying to stay in their own spots. Even Shay has moved out of the house. I miss them all but sometimes being missed is a lot better than a person always getting on your nerves.*
>
> *Mama's baby D.A., I always miss his little chunky monkey butt. He is getting so big that I don't want to miss anything that he does in life or in his baby stages. His smile is amazing. I love him more than life itself. He is an amazing gift from God.*

But trouble developed soon enough. Katina's father, Ernest, had learned that Lindsay was strip-teasing. Calling her father by his name, as she usually did, Katina wrote:

> *My whole family are back stabbers to the fullest. I'm the blame for all that goes wrong on a daily basis.*
>
> *How in the world did Ernest know that Lindsay was dancing? Of course Lindsay knows that it was my sister Lisa and Boobie's dumb ass. I sat down and thought long and hard about 'my family.' I feel as though I have to bury my family and start over from scratch. Like build my own family, a sister and a few brothers.*
>
> *I have to stay clean and keep my head clear 'cause some strange things go through my head. I'm not about to let other people shut or tear me down. I have nothing to prove to anyone.*

After struggling with menial jobs, it was back to the old ways of making money—escorting. Again she didn't have to do the 60/40 thing and could keep all of her earnings. In nine days she made about $1,400. Katina confessed it was scary, though, having to get a room and never know who's coming and what his plans are.

So far I have been lucky and watched over by GOD.

I have this one guy who is already a regular. I have had some strange clients. I think this one white man thinks that we go together. He told me he has a wife but he's looking for a girlfriend. I have one man who likes licking female toes.

He said he would pay $200 a week to lick my feet. I don't judge people, but damn that's crazy.

I witnessed the craziest shit ever. I actually saw a man do a line of coke. He offered some to me but, you know, the kid don't get down like that AT ALL. I'm so proud of myself not feeling other people's pressure of doing the drugs of their choice. The shit had this muthafucka looking quite crazy.

Shit, I can barely handle weed. I know I can't do that bullshit.

And then:

Surprised myself on this day. The girls and me and D.A. went to church with my boyfriend. It was nice 'cause we haven't been to church in a long time. I didn't understand the service, but it felt good just being in his house. Afterwards we went to Golden Corral to eat.

For a while, there was peace in the family. Katina couldn't stand it when her kids were mad at each other. She wished they understood that they were a team. Rod-Ni was now 19 and seemed to have changed overnight. She was at that age when older guys could persuade her to do certain things, telling her what she wanted to hear.

Lindsay, on the other hand, seemed to have grown up since becoming a mother. Katina was proud of her. Shay, too, was growing up, but not in all the right ways.

You know I wanna say this, I really don't approve of them escorting. All of us. That's some Oprah shit. I want all of us to stop.

Old habits die hard, though. Katina started doing discreet massaging, as she called it, and started taking on a lot of clients. Most of her calls came in the middle of the night.

However, demand for her girls at the university had waned.

On April 8, 2013, the Cardinals made a furious comeback to beat Michigan and win the NCAA basketball tournament 82-76. The triumph made Pitino the first Division 1 basketball coach to win the title with two different schools.

It was a boost for the University of Louisville and a boost for Pitino as well. For nearly three years the cloud of scandal had hung over him because of his sexual encounter in 2003 with a woman who later married one of Pitino's employees. Although the matter was more or less settled in 2010, any lingering taint had now been banished.

Coincidentally or not, McGee's request for dancers also had diminished. On April 9th, Powell texted McGee:

> Powell: U know my girls wanna see the players before they leave... so if it's possible can u set something up wen y'all get home... Please.

On May 16, 2013 she complained in a text:

> Powell: Wats up you really don't fuck wit us no more.

In June, Katina got an answer—an important potential recruit.

Been a long time since we've been up to U of L to do a show. McGee texted me like, what's up? He wanted me to bring three girls up there for a new recruit named JaQuan Lyle, he and his friend. I took Rod-Ni, TooTall, Jazmine and Shay, who calls herself Sammi. TooTall made $100, Shay made $100, and

Jazzy made nothing because she did absolutely nothing.
They was still pumped up about winning the championship,
wanted us to do it for free (never that!).

Lyle, a point guard from Evansville, Indiana, signed with Louisville but de-committed and in 2015 signed with Ohio State. The message exchange between Katina and McGee leading up to this totaled 22 texts.

We saw Montrezl Harrell, and a new guy named Chris.
It's crazy 'cause since the championship they have gotten so
cocky. Like they used to be the nicest people, but now they
are feeling themselves.

Afterwards we saw Chane Behanan, he was going to an all-
white party. He reminded me that his b-day is Sept. 24, so he
wants a show. McGee said that I had given his money back he
would give me the signed Maker's Mark bottle by Rick Pitino,
and it's gonna be worth something in 15 years. But I'm cool.
So until next time.

Two days later, Katina asked McGee in a text:

Powell: Hey Andre what was the name of the recruit that the tall chic was with Saturday?

McGee: jaquan lyles... some other dudes is looking for tall chick.

This is a reference to a dancer named TooTall. She was especially popular for a specialty trick that men found particularly exciting.

New business came from elsewhere for a time.

In July, 2013 Katina wrote from the escort scene:

Unbelievable. I had a client today, an old white man.
He wanted me to be his little nigga bitch. I tell ya, white
people trip me the fuck out. A bunch of nigga lovers.
So far in a day I made $1,000, no kidding. I had some good

clients and I had some ridiculous clients today. In the end I had one client, he was kind of young, that worked for the Galt House. It was 5 a.m. and I didn't know what to expect. I seriously thought when the session was over that he was gonna stick me up for the money. But he was a perfect gentleman.

Next, Rod-Ni and Shay went to the Courtyard Marriott for two men met through the Universal Soul Circus. One man gave Shay $80 for sexual services. He was a midget. Rod-Ni did her business (with the other man) while his son was there.

Meanwhile, Katina made $540 on an unusual trip to Elizabethtown, Kentucky. She explained:

Finally the couple thing. These people have been asking me to come to E-Town for a lady named Wilma. She was around 60 years old. She was cute to be an older woman.

It was crazy 'cause this man controlled this woman so much that it was scary. They asked me to put on some lingerie and I agreed. She wouldn't do anything without him. I was so nervous that it was beyond crazy. Once the session was over (a whole two hours) I was relieved. I don't think I wanna do that again.

Escorting, it seemed, occupied so much of Katina's time, there wasn't time for dance outings. In August, she wrote:

I have so many girls that want me to put them on or help them out. I told you bitches the clubs ain't poppin' at all. So far I've had Miss Jay, Precious, Ne-Ne and a few others that wanna make something crack in Louisville. So far the only thing that's working for me is stupid ass BP (Backpage). The shit is so addictive that it's sickening. I wish I could help everybody but I can't.

Although there were no dance outings at the University of Louisville, several of the players and former players were around.

On August 13:

T-Will came to town for a few days and called McGee to get in touch with Rod-Ni. He's been wanting Rod-Ni since the beginning of time. Well, I don't know what happened but he changed his mind. So I'm asleep and Rod-Ni comes in.

My phone goes off with a number I've never seen before.

So Rod-Ni's like, T-Will's gonna call you. I'm like for what?

She said I don't know; he's gonna call you though.

Now here's how he starts the conversation. 'What's up?

I heard you're the queen of high prices?' I'm like, what?

He was like, 'yeah, do you wanna come see me?' I get there, Courtyard Marriott. I'm up stairs and the door was cracked. So I stood in the doorway 'till he got back. He asked me for a massage. I massaged his back, then he pulled down his shorts and asked me to massage his ass. That just blew me away. Another nigga who wants a bitch to play with their ass.

Shit is getting crazy.

Rod-Ni was mad at Katina because she took the call from T-Will. Her daughter was just star-struck, she reasoned. Katina saw things different than her daughter.

I don't see none of these fools as a catch. I look at them as banks. My feelings are personal.

I don't like sharing them with any of these jerks.

Katina wanted to stop posting on Backpage. She wrote:

It's getting crazy and real....just too much to it all.

Nothing crazy has happened and I knock on wood. Thank you, Jesus. It's just my time to bow out of this. Plus I miss my Shay.

But listen to this. I had a client yesterday, he was white, sexy as fuck. He wanted a massage. We talked about professional shit. We smoked a blunt and when it came time to get a massage he was like, baby girl, I'm good, but you can keep the money. Then called the next morning and asked me did I wanna go to breakfast. Fuck, NAW!!

At the end of August, McGee wanted dancers. Katina sent a text:

Powell: Whats up mcgee? Do you still need us today?

McGee: Yessssssssssssssssssssssssssssss. I need the whole show!!

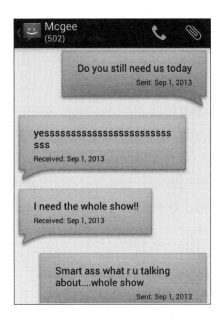

As Katina explained in her diary:

McGee called and asked if I could bring two females up to U of L to 'take care of' two new recruits and a parent who is visiting. Later he called and said he needed a whole show. I'm like, nigga, make up your damn mind. He was like, I really want y'all to do this show for Earl Clark but Coach is talking their heads off. So bottom line we didn't do the show. Would have been nice to see Earl Clark $$$.

Clark was a former Louisville star who played for the Brooklyn Nets and other teams in the NBA.

Often McGee and Katina would go into another room and sit and talk about the pressure he was under while the side-deals were going on.

At the last U of L show McGee confided in Katina:

> McGee said shit has really changed up there. Players
> ain't listening or taking this game serious. SAD!! He was
> depressed. He didn't feel he had control. It was written all
> over his face.

The text exchange between McGee and Katina included a change in time, because, McGee said, "Coach is talking they head to death... might be too late."

Meantime, Katina had trouble, again, with Shay.

Katina got a call from Shay, hearing a disturbing conversation Shay was having with a man:

> She called me one day and said, 'Mama, listen to this.' ...
> 'Dude, that's glass that got on me.' Then I heard him say,
> 'Bitch, if you kick me I will be the last person you ever kick.'
> Then the phone went blank.
>
> She told me he hit her twice in her head and almost broke her
> leg. I panicked like crazy.
>
> Shay was in Texas. She managed to take his truck and get to a
> Greyhound station.
>
> When she got back (to Louisville) she told me the most
> unbelievable stories.
>
> Lambo is the pimp's name, 29 from Houston. He has eight
> hos, as they would say. Drives a green Hummer. He beats on
> his girls, hits them with belts, his fists. Makes them stand on
> corners for hours. One girl they said got shot in her head for
> him. She has tubes in her stomach and can't work. One girl is

17. They work the track, the strip clubs and the hotels.
One room to sleep, one room to work out of.

Since she has been back I have learned so much about the
prostitution game that I never really knew existed.

The craziest thing is she's not ashamed to talk about it.
She said what her and these girls had in common was they all
had no fathers. One man took eight girls and promised them a
bunch of bullshit and (gave them) a beating full of threats that
scared them into staying.

Soon, Katina was able to focus on business again. She agreed to do a bachelor party at the barber shop for a friend of Tink's.

The bachelor was cool but Tink went down on a dancer.
It shocked me that he did that in front of me because we are
intimate and more than friends. The guy (sponsor—who
was the best man) *kept grabbing me saying stay in here*
with us. I asked Lola (stripper I knew) to give him a private
lap dance, Why he wanted me in there I know, but at the
same time I'll never know. Now all of a sudden he won't stop
texting me. He texts every morning. I think it's cute but crazy.
I got the money, so that's all that mattered.

The money kept flowing. On November 1 Katina got a call from a white girl.

She wanted to surprise her fiancé with 'me.' How nice. I made
$350. When I say he was shocked, it was the real kind.
He pulled out damn near $5,000 in rubber bands. She was
cool and tasted good, I might add.

As 2013 wound down Katina summarized where things stood in her business.

Unfortunately, some of her personnel were out of commission.

Almost the end of the year. Most of the chicks that danced

in my shows, okay, now some of them are pregnant. That is
crazy. They screamed about how gay they were, 'Oh, my God,
he just touched my no no.' Now some of them are pregnant?!
They told me they were gay!

But all in all, Katina celebrated that she'd made "so much money" escorting in 2013. She'd met many strange people asking for strange things. Threesomes. Requests to urinate in her mouth. All kinds of clients, too—businessmen, thugs and meth dealers. She told herself she was ready to find permanent work with benefits.

Despite lofty intentions, Katina decided to energize her escort business. She wanted to do a show in which the dancers would be Beyoncé look-alikes. She wanted to do a documentary about prostitutes, escorts, call girls and madams.

She had an idea for hair and makeup products that glowed.

She thought about an obstacle course people might find challenging.

She had someone draw a design of an "IND" bracelet to keep girls safe (I'm N Danger).

And the big news: Rod-Ni was pregnant.

I'm happy but at the same time I'm sad. She's a really good
girl and maybe this is what God wanted her for. She's gonna
be a really good mommy.....2 grandkids already. OH MY GOD!!

"RICK REALLY NEEDS THIS KID SO MAKE IT HAPPEN."

-Katina Powell quoting Andre McGee

Out of the blue, on March 3, 2014, Katina exchanged text messages with McGee.

Powell: Wats up we cant get a hey or nothin can we us really didn't fuck wit us...that's cool

McGee: yoooo... where y'all been

Powell: Been texting u... u didn't fuck with us.

McGee: Man..this probably my last year here

Powell: Why wat happened

McGee: theres no promotion in the near future so I gotta make some moves.

Powell: Awww don't go... I wanna c.u.

McGee: No birthday love?

Powell: Happy bday we love us... call me

In fact, McGee was about to leave. On April 21 it was announced that he was taking an assistant coach's position at the University of Missouri/Kansas City, where he would work

under Kareem Richardson, a former assistant coach at Louisville.

Chane Behanan also was leaving the city of Louisville.
A week earlier, Behanan and Powell had a lengthy exchange of text messages.

> Powell: If U need something let me know,

> Behanan: Bet

He was not picked in the NBA draft that year, but was selected for the league's development draft.

Oddly, she missed the announcement about McGee's change of jobs, busy with escort activities.

> *Bachelor party for some big guy who was getting married. I let Lindsay, Lola and J.J. dance. Rod-Ni handled the business part and I got paid ($400). Another guy that was there called and asked me to do a bachelor party in June.*

And another:

> *Did a bachelor party for another friend of Tink's ($300). I took Rod-Ni, Lindsay, J.J. and T-Mama. The bachelor gave away $50 to the coldest female (the best). It was a big chick, she was good to be a big girl, and I was like a kid in a candy shop running upstairs to tell the girls everything she did. She could do a lot of tricks with a peeled banana in her mouth with whipped cream dripping. She had a lot of props like a dominatrix whip.*

On July 22, 2014, Katina heard a voice from the past.

> *I received a phone call from Andre McGee. He said he was in Kansas coaching. I was shocked to hear from him. He asked if myself and another girl would do him a favor. So I did! $500 total. He said that they really needed this kid Antonio Blakeney, he's supposed to be the top pick in the world.*

It was him and his (guardian). Before we hung up he said,
'Rick really wants this kid, so make it happen.' Of course
Andre always made it more dramatic than it was, but this time
he sounded as though he needed me to put the special sauce
on this kid and his (guardian).

At the time, Louisville was in a "battle" with arch-rival Kentucky to sign the player, sensational shooting guard Antonio Blakeney of Sarasota, Florida. Blakeney, who had visited Louisville earlier, returned for exhibition games July 23-26 at the Kentucky Exposition Center for the American Athletic Union Super Showcase, part of a program to allow student athletes to maximize their national exposure.

Katina said,

At about 7 o'clock I went to the basketball dorm and a light-
skinned guy came out. He was sexy as hell and I had never seen
this guy before. I didn't see him as a player, I saw him as another
one of the team's flunkies. He gave me $200 in twenties, shook
my hand, and walked away, almost as if he didn't want me to get
a good look at him. I got the money and left.

Meanwhile, she called Shay.

I asked her was she down to make some money, and she said
yes. I picked up Shay and we rode out to a hotel on Whipps
Mill Road, about 25 minutes from where we lived. (Embassy
Suites). We went up to Room 328 and knocked on the door
and Antonio opened the door. He looked like he was growing
dreadlocks, something like a small afro just starting. He was
in the front room and in the back room was his (guardian)
standing in the doorway. He had on white shorts and a white
shirt. He was a little taller than me and on the chubby side.

We introduced ourselves and Antonio directed me to the back
bedroom while he and Shay stayed in the living room.

Katina's journal identified the man as his uncle but Antonio told Shay the man was his father.

> *He sat on the bed and I asked him if he was enjoying his time here in Louisville. He said yes with a slight smile. I asked him what did he like about Louisville. He said the Yum Center, the players, and the 'hospitality' that the coaches have shown him. I asked him if Antonio was coming to Louisville. He smiled and said it depends. I knew then it was time to get started.*

Afterward, as Katina was getting dressed, she asked again if Antonio would be signing on the dotted line. He responded that with all they'd received, how could he say no? She noticed that Shay and Antonio were sitting on the couch and talking after they had sex. Katina asked Antonio if he would be signing to Louisville. He said yes.

> *I noticed when we were leaving that there was a whole basketball team in the lobby. They looked as though they might have been a high school team but these guys were way too tall. We looked at one another, laughed, and left the hotel.*

What she didn't know was that Antonio slid his number to Shay to call him at a later date, and she did (the next day), this time serving (both Antonio and a coach) and not getting paid. "*It's called taking one for the team,*" she said.

A few hours later Andre called and asked how it went. She told him they were done and that he'd be signing. McGee was shocked at how fast Katina and Shay got in and out, but by then they'd had plenty of practice, of course.

> *He asked me for my government name and address and told me that in the morning I could go to any Walmart and pick up the rest of my money ($300). When I got to the Walmart the lady at the counter looked at the money-gram and said, Hey I know this name, Andre McGee. Don't he play for U of L?*

The reference Katina made to Whipps Mill Road is to one of the outer drives around the Embassy Suites. As phone records show, McGee had sent her the actual address, 9940 Corporate Campus Drive.

Phone records show that on July 22, 2014, McGee called and/or texted Katina nine times and she called/texted him eight times. The calls between 6:08 p.m. and 11:11 p.m., totaled about 35 minutes. All of McGee's calls were from a California number. It is not known what he was doing there, although he is originally from the area.

There were two exchanges the following day. It is not known who asked McGee to arrange the liaison, or who bankrolled it. The fact that someone connected in some way at the University of Louisville knew that McGee—now at a smaller school more than 500 miles away—could arrange for prostitutes makes it clear this person or persons knew about McGee's activities while he still was on the Louisville payroll.

On September 4, 2014, Blakeney committed to Louisville, but changed his mind 11 days later and eventually went to Louisiana State University.

In late August 2015, at the publisher's request, Katina's daughter

Shay sent an Instagram message to Antonio Blakeney in hopes that editors would be able to reach him for a response. She asked him if he recalled meeting her at the Embassy Suites in Louisville.

He replied "Yea I do wassup?" She asked for his cell phone number. He did not reply. She did not disclose why she was making the inquiry.

Blakeney's mother, speaking on her son's behalf, said that Antonio denied he was ever at the Embassy Suites.

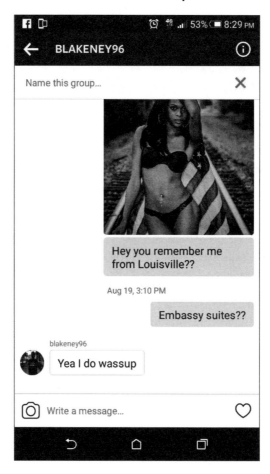

**MISTAKES ARE ALWAYS FORGIVABLE,
IF ONE HAS THE COURAGE TO ADMIT THEM.**

-Andre McGee tweet, @DreTheCoach

Dre the Coach—Andre McGee—isn't talking, for now, anyway.

McGee did not respond to three requests for an interview. Two were made by telephone, one by email to his mailbox at the University of Missouri, Kansas City (UMKC). A second email was sent, with attachment, asking McGee to identify a man in a photograph. Again there was no response.

Paul Puryear, better known as Tink, the barber and Cardinal fan who arranged the first two dormitory parties, agreed to an interview by telephone but cut it off upon the first question.

Kareem Richardson, a former assistant at Louisville and now, as head basketball coach at UMKC, McGee's boss, did not respond to two messages.

Louisville Coach Rick Pitino, through a spokesman, said that based on a limited summary provided to him, he was unaware of any instances of players or recruits being exposed to strippers or hookers.

The spokesman said a survey of athletic department employees, based on the limited information, turned up no indication of anyone possessing pertinent information.

The University of Louisville officials say they've launched an investigation and released this statement. "The University of Louisville has retained an outside expert to investigate allegations evidently contained in a book that IBJ Book Publishing, LLC has been asked to publish. The outside expert is aggressively reviewing this situation in full cooperation with relevant authorities, including the NCAA. The university notes that the publisher has provided sparse detail to date and repeats its request for additional detail in order to further the thoroughness of the investigation. If the investigation uncovers any misconduct by University employees, the university will deal with it swiftly and severely."

Chane Behanan, who recently played for the Reno Bighorns, declined an interview request and, upon a second request, hung up. He lives in Cincinnati.

Montrezl Harrell said that he didn't know anything about the dorm parties arranged by Andre McGee.

An attorney representing Antonio Blakeney returned a call on his behalf but did not have a comment.

For the most part, other former Cardinal players who were students at the time that events in this book occurred, either did not respond to messages, including Facebook or Twitter, or could not be reached for comment. Some are playing overseas. Attempts to reach several recruits also were unsuccessful.

Three former players who answered questions said they were unaware of the dorm visits.

Allegations about sex and recruiting are hardly new. "Cheap sex, cheaper beer and male sports participation have locked themselves in a bunker deeper and more secure than anything Saddam Hussein could imagine," columnist Jason Whitlock wrote on ESPN.com. "The locker room is America's last X-rated playground for men."

In 2002, the NCAA put the University of Alabama on probation for a number of violations, including allegations that players used strippers to perform for recruits.

In 2003, the father of running back Lynell Hamilton said his son was offered alcohol and sex during a visit to the University of Oregon. Young Hamilton went on to play at San Diego State.

That same year, a key football recruit said he wouldn't attend the University of Minnesota after players took him to a strip club.

In 2004, the owner of a Denver striptease company said players from a number of universities, including the University of Colorado and the University of Nevada Las Vegas, had hired girls for recruiting parties.

"Obviously, parties that involve sex and alcohol to lure recruits and end in sexual assault are intolerable, not to mention illegal, beginning perhaps with underage drinking," then U.S. Rep Clifford Stearns of Florida complained during a 2004 congressional hearing on college recruiting.

"Allegations of the use of prostitutes, sex parties, booze, drugs and late nights at strip clubs have popped up all over the place," said U.S. Rep Diana DeGette of Colorado, referring to a list of 22 alleged recruiting violations from around the country culled from media reports alone. She added: "Think of how many allegations there are that have not been put to light in the press."

The case of the University of Louisville appears to be unprecedented in terms of frequency, duration and variety, dealing as it does with part of the men's dormitory, a basketball assistant's private condominium, and various hotels in the Louisville area.

If only a portion of the encounters happened as interviews and records suggest they did, it raises important questions about supervision, player policy, dorm oversight, security, rules enforcement, and, for that matter, the standards of culture and attitude that should hold sway in a major educational institution.

Over the years in question, Louisville had approximately eight assistant coaches. It is unclear what their relationship was with McGee.

Perhaps most intriguing is who at Louisville would have contacted McGee, when McGee was working in another state, and at the time was in California, to ask him to arrange cross-country for two women to visit a potential recruit and his guardian at a Louisville hotel?

Who would have repaid to McGee the $300 he wired to Katina?

Who was the mystery man who, Katina says, came out of the dormitory to hand her $200 cash, just as McGee had promised?

As much as Katina and some of the other women knew or witnessed, none of them knew where the cash really came from. Were there—or are there—boosters with deep pockets who want to see the Cardinals win at any cost, especially in competition with the super-rival University of Kentucky?

Perhaps as many people might wonder why Katina decided to try to write a book. Money, of course, was one reason. And what else?

"I wanted to say something a year ago, but the pressure that was on me was very scary and I didn't want to get Andre in any trouble. I had people telling me that if I told my story my life would be put in danger, so I just kept quiet and didn't say anything."

Nevertheless, it is clear that a turning-point came when, she says, McGee and an unidentified man told her they wanted her to bring white women to the dorm. The request obviously angered Katina, but not because of racism. She had taken pride in the variety of black women she could deliver, and she saw the request as an insult to everything she'd done up to that point.

Katina came to an Indianapolis publisher because she feared no publisher in Louisville would take on the project. Before contacting IBJ Book Publishing, which she found through a Google search, she says she called the NCAA headquarters in Indianapolis. She says she was told no one there could take a complaint against a large university over the phone because it's hearsay.

In recent months, her attitude about what happened, and her own role, has changed markedly.

"People should be aware of not only what goes on at a university, but

what these kids are persuaded and influenced with. What kid would not choose a university that provides drugs, sex and alcohol? I often wondered what if one of these girls got pregnant, or if one of these players had gotten a girl pregnant. How would that be explained to a parent?"

"This was a full-time, under the table, hush-hush job for me. I started feeling some sort of commitment to Andre and the team, until they started putting a lot of pressure on me. Andre was feeling it the most. Andre was very loyal to Pitino, and I was loyal to Andre."

Her life has changed as well. She says she's finished with the sex trade in all aspects. She's using her entrepreneurial gifts to start a business to shuttle people without transportation to job interviews. She and her boyfriend love each other and are working on their complicated fifteen year relationship. Two of her daughters, Lindsay and Rod-Ni, also have changed, getting normal jobs or going to school.

The University of Louisville recently reported two minor violations to the NCAA, one for giving six basketball players $7 each to play laser-tag.

EPILOGUE

I DANCED ONE TIME AT THE DORM. I SLEPT WITH ONE
(PLAYER); IT WAS A THREESOME. I WAS ALL ABOUT
THE MONEY, AND I MADE THE BEST OF IT. BEING A
MOTHER, I'M LOOKING FOR JOBS. IF I GOT ANOTHER
SIDE-DEAL CALL, I WOULD DO IT.

-Honey

Sometimes a perfectly ordinary day will unexpectedly lead to perfectly extraordinary things.

On a perfectly ordinary spring day in 2015...

...five women, including Katina Powell, gathered at a private meeting room in the old Louisville Public Library, not far from downtown, to recount their experiences with basketball players and recruits from the University of Louisville.

All of the women were single. Two of them brought their young children. They were as nervous as they were curious. It had to seem unusual, even surreal, that now, out of the blue, a year or two after the fact, anyone would be interested in what they did on several or many evenings at a hallowed educational institution not far away.

Or perhaps they were nervous and curious because a writer and publisher had arrived from Indianapolis and were interested in their stories.

After all, some of the women hadn't graduated from high school. They had children out of wedlock. They'd received welfare or other public benefits. It was obvious, even if they didn't admit it (as some did) that getting money to live and raise their kids was a challenge virtually every day.

As they talked, it became clear they weren't confessing or apologizing. Probably neither of these things occurred to anyone. The tone and words were matter-of-fact: The stripteases and other activities had been fun, at times exciting. They'd met interesting, influential people, NBA players. They'd made a lot of money, although, of course, never enough.

"I was all about the money, and I made the best of it," said Honey, 28 and three months pregnant. *"Being a mother, I'm looking for jobs. If I got another side-deal call, I would do it."* Her son, Princeton, climbed off her lap and waved for attention.

Of course Honey was there because of Katina. Shrewd, ambitious, opportunistic Katina originally had brought the group together half a decade ago, coached and mothered them through dozens of parties and other events, put in their hands a lot of money they otherwise wouldn't have.

And now, amazingly, Katina was trying to assemble a book about her life. What had been private or secret for so long now would be very, very public.

In future days, the writer and publisher would talk to other women who had danced in the nude and done other things, and, like her, their attitude and tone was matter-of-fact, without even the smallest hint that whatever they did was anything other than naughty, just girls taking care of boys for money they could use for rent, groceries, formula, weed and cigarettes.

But three of the women were Katina's daughters, and they knew that the sex business has a dark, perverse side hardly as pretty as entertaining college and high school kids in the buffed sanctuary of a college dorm. Of course the four of them had shared confidences, laughed at incidents that would make other mothers cringe, argued, hugged, and dreamed together.

Now her daughters—Shay would arrive late—were telling all to strangers with pens, note pads and a tape recorder.

Lindsay, 23 and pregnant with her second child, had danced under the name Brittany.

"Guys (the players) were cocky," she said. *"I didn't like them. Some were nice. Some had girlfriends. Guys would pick which girls they*

96

wanted. I like to dance. It was fun. McGee gave me an outfit because I didn't have enough clothes on (to start with). I still have the sweat pants. I felt sorry for him because he 'needed' recruits."

Rod-Ni, 22, had her daughter, Cali Marie, with her. She said:

"I liked Andre a lot. He always tried to hit on me. He had just graduated when we met him. I thought if this is Andre McGee's dorm and that is what he wanted to do, then that's OK. I saw him last a year ago, or right before he left. He was pressured by someone he reported to."

There was small talk until friends waiting in the hallway signaled Shay's arrival. It was like a warning alarm.

Earlier, Katina had remembered an episode which epitomized risks Shay took.

"Shay hadn't answered her phone. So when Lindsay called her back later, a guy answered from Durham, North Carolina. He said he had seen a guy in a white car get out, slam the phone, get back in the car and speed off. He said it seems as though she's in trouble.

"We instantly panicked and asked what happened. He called the police and they called me. I didn't know what was going on. (Later) Shay said a man tried to attack her, so she locked herself in the bathroom and screamed to the top of her lungs. I am so grateful for the guy who found the phone and the officers on the job.

"She doesn't understand how dangerous and close she was to losing her life once again. She thinks this is a joke. She meets this guy at random and thinks he can make her a super-star. I don't know what else to do about it."

Now, before a sullen and defiant Shay came through the door, one of the dancers warned: *"Watch out for her. She's evil."*

It didn't sound as if she meant evil in any moral sense. It was more a synonym for trouble.

Everyone looked at Katina.

"Yes," she said, *"she's evil."*

Her eyes were filled with frustration, tenderness, love, and, perhaps, regret.

Shay, 20, smart, hard-edged but seemingly self-confident, described in detail an encounter she and her mother had had with a potential recruit and his guardian. She thought the player was too young. The player mistakenly believed he was getting a freebie. She and the player had met again the next day and smoked a few blunts. She had sex with the player's coach, and he also failed to pay.

She didn't like to dance but went to some of the dorm parties. She'd had sex with one player four times.

"I want a rich man and a wedding ring," she said, half-jokingly.

She talked briefly with her mother, and walked away to a perilous future, the only penalty Katina had paid for her years in the sex trade.

APPENDIX

THE CARDINAL RULES

NCAA RULES

Title: 91.1.1. - Severe Breach of Conduct (Level 1 Violation)

A severe breach of conduct is one or more violations that seriously undermine or threaten the integrity of the NCAA Collegiate Model, as set forth in the constitution and bylaws, including any violation that provides or is intended to provide a substantial or extensive recruiting, competitive or other advantage, or a substantial or impermissible benefit. Among other examples, the following, in appropriate circumstances, may constitute a severe breach of conduct: (Adopted 10/30/12 effective 8/1/13, Revised: 7/13/14)

(a) Lack of institutional control;

(b) Academic misconduct;

(c) Failure to cooperate in an NCAA enforcement investigation;

(d) Individual unethical or dishonest conduct, regardless of whether the underlying institutional violations are considered Level 1;

(e) A bylaw 11.1.1.1 violation by a head coach resulting from an underlying violation by an individual within the sports program;

(f) Cash payment or other benefits provided by a coach, administrator or representative of the institution's athletics interests intended to secure, or which resulted in, enrollment of a prospective student-athlete;

(g) Third-party involvement in recruiting violations in which institutional officials knew or should have known about the involvement;

(h) Intentional violations or reckless indifference to the NCAA constitution and bylaws; or

(i) Collective Level II and/or Level III violations.

Source: www.ncaa.org

ABOUT DICK CADY

Dick Cady worked for the Dearborn (Michigan) Guide, Ypsilanti Daily Press, Detroit News, Indianapolis Star and Newsday and also wrote for The Nation, NUVO Newsweekly, Indianapolis Monthly Magazine, the Johnson County Journal and Bloomington Herald-Times. He won 51 local, state and national journalism awards, including the Pulitzer Prize for special local reporting, the Associated Press Freedom of Information Award, the Drew Pearson Award, George Polk Memorial Award, Sigma Delta Chi national journalism society Gold Medal, an American Bar Association special certificate of merit, and two National Headliners awards. In 1976-77 he was assistant director of "The Arizona Project" sponsored by Investigative Reporters and Editors, which examined organized crime, political corruption and land fraud after the assassination of Phoenix reporter Don Bolles. The project won a special gold medal from Sigma Delta Chi as "the outstanding investigative reporting effort of the year." Cady is the author of six books.